THE INVISIBLE STORY

The Perfect Tool for Sci-Fi & Fantasy Writers

By David Kochenderfer

The Invisible Story:
The Perfect Tool for Sci-Fi & Fantasy Writers

ISBN: 978–0–9816171–6–9
1. Writing   2. Homeschooling   3. Language Arts
4. Authorship   5. Composition & Creative Writing

Cover and Interior Design by Spring Moon

FIRST EDITION

Printed in the United States of America

For additional orders contact Rebecca@Homeschool.com

Homeschool.com, Inc.
12210 Herdal Drive, Suite 11
Auburn, CA 95603 USA

This book is dedicated to every science fiction and fantasy writer and to every story that was never written.

The Invisible Story is a book that is waiting to be written by you. Right now, the story is only in your imagination. But as you fill in these pages, it becomes visible, and the world you always imagined will be brought to life.

Your Book Title

Your Artwork

By:

Your Name

NOTES

1 _____

2 _____

3 _____

4 _____

5 _____

6 _____

7 _____

- _____

- _____

- _____

- _____

- _____

- _____

- _____

NOTES

_____   _____

_____   _____

_____   _____

_____   _____

_____   _____

_____   _____

_____   _____

○ _____

☽ _____

★ _____

+ _____

– _____

A _____

Ω _____

What does your world look like?

Your Artwork

CHAPTER 1

Chapter Title

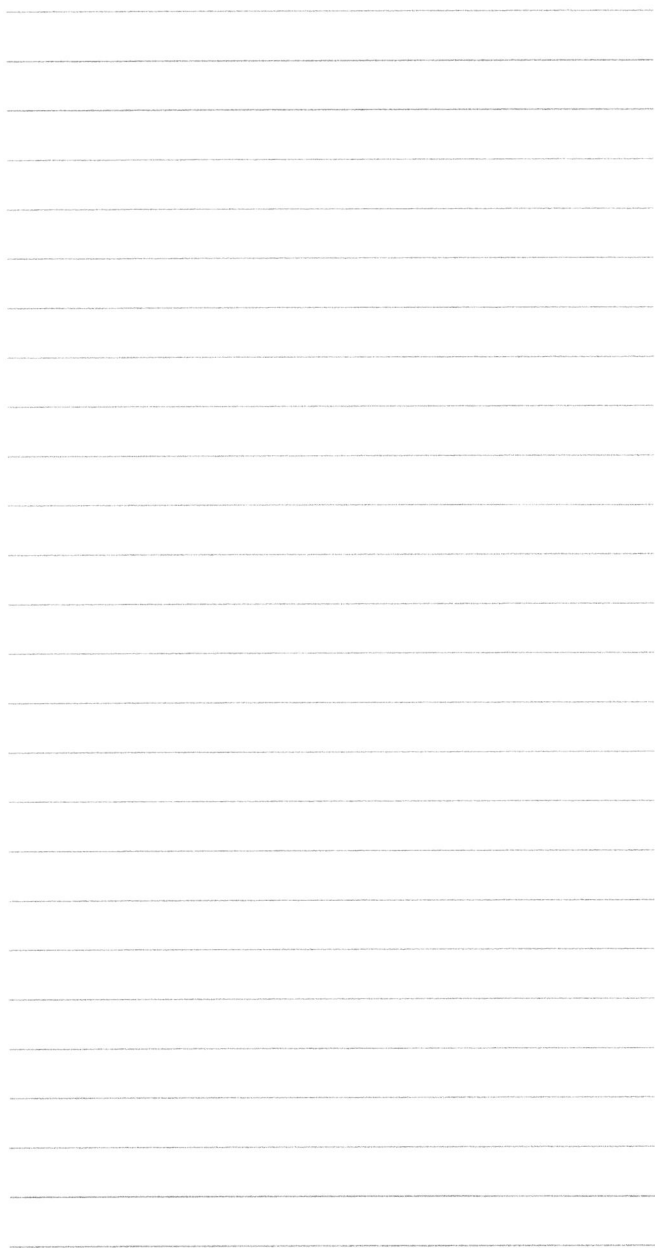

"Allow absolutely nothing to hamper you
or hold you up in any way."

— Eileen Caddy

Your Artwork

CHAPTER 2

Chapter Title

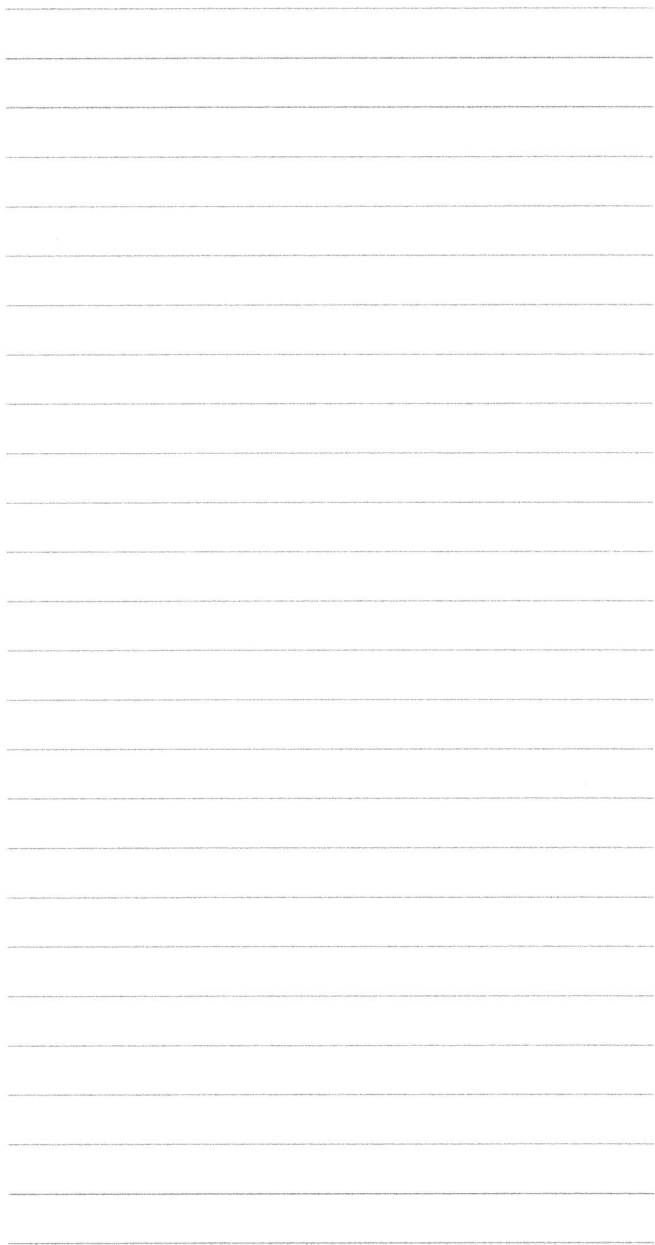

14

"There is no such thing as bad writing. The only bad writer is one who leaves their ideas unwritten. "

— D.K.

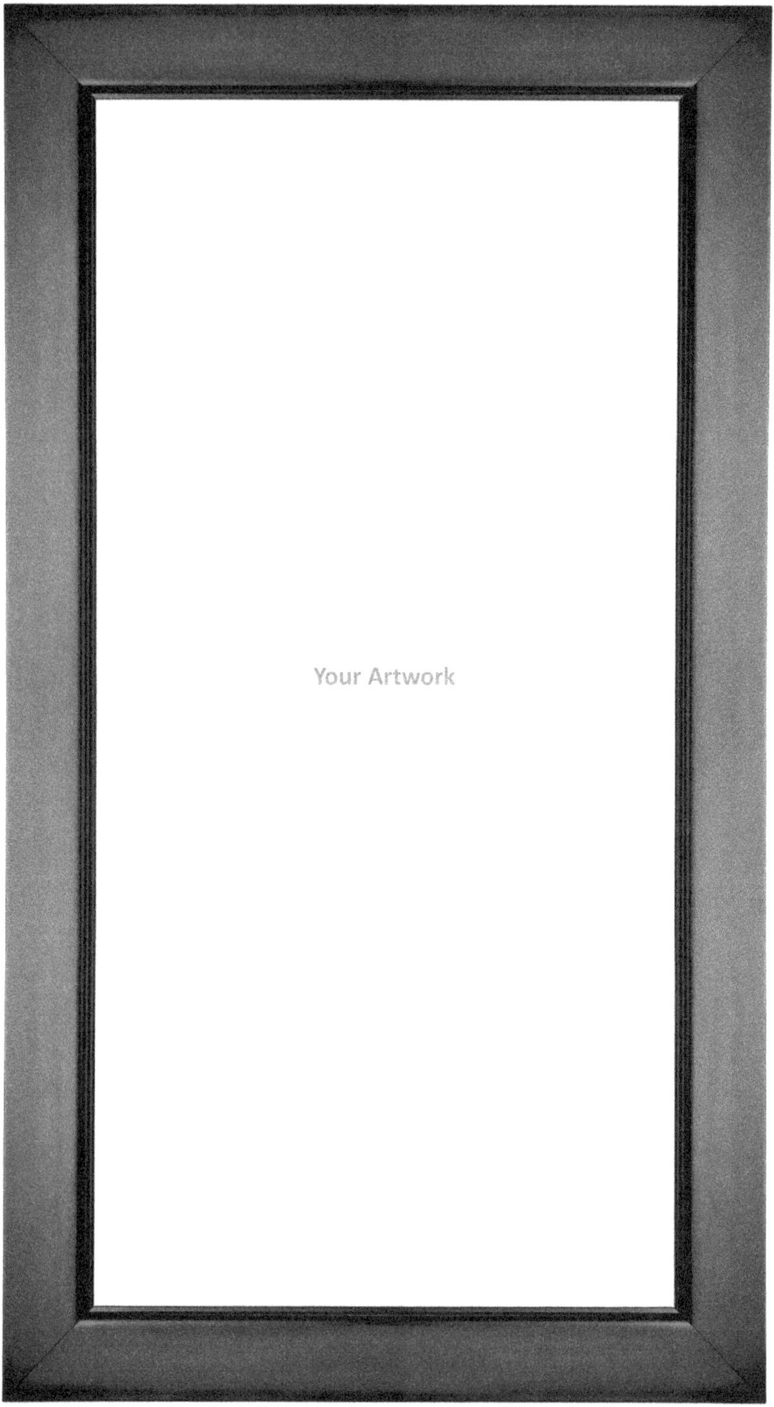
Your Artwork

CHAPTER 3

Chapter Title

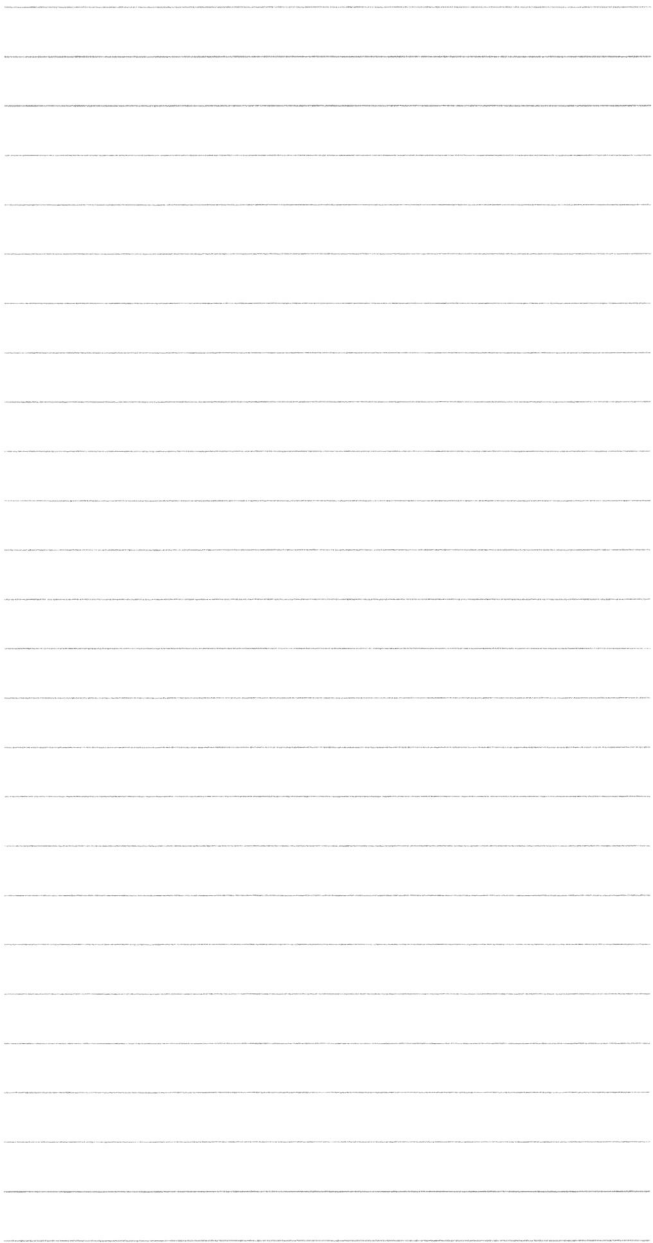

"Set your sights higher, the higher the better, and
let your imagination do the rest. "

– D.K.

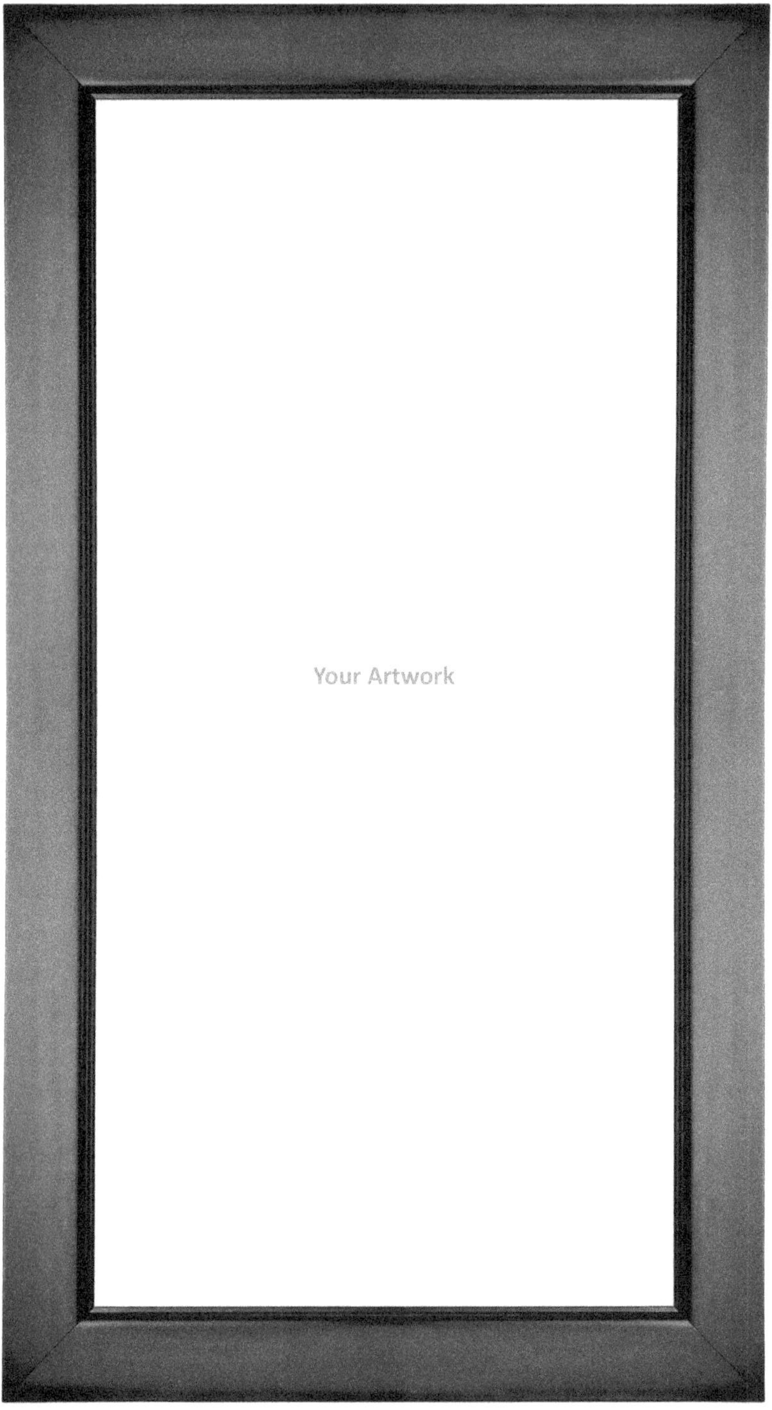
Your Artwork

CHAPTER 4

Chapter Title

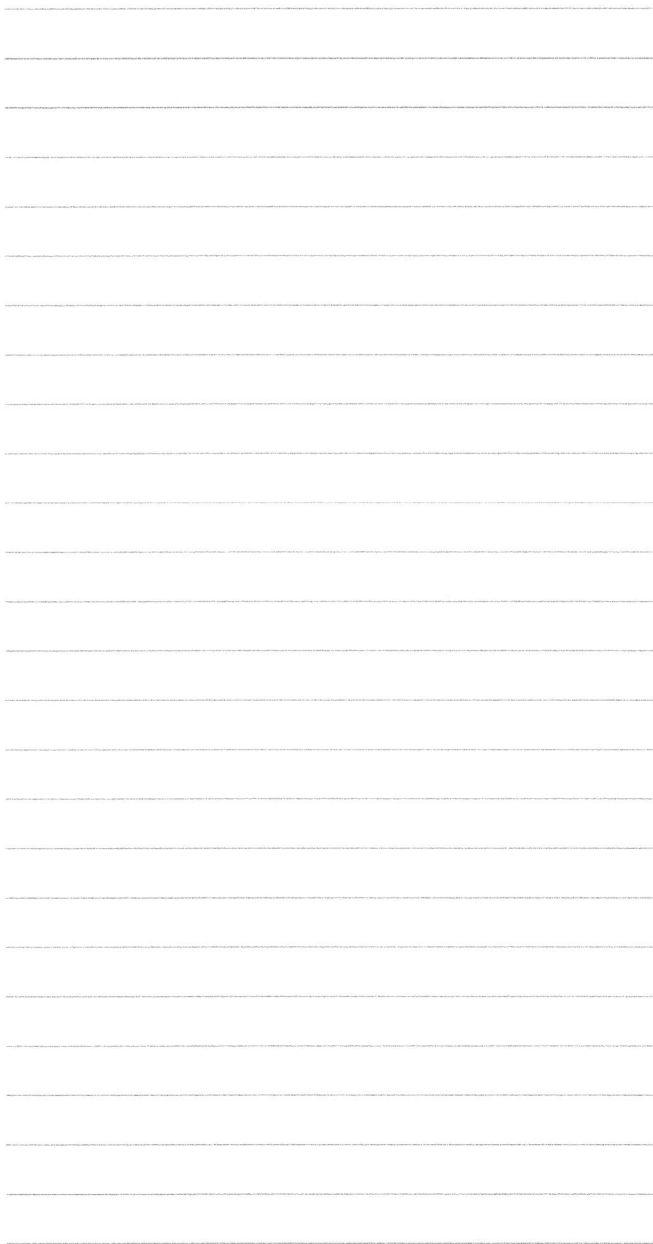

"Ideas by themselves are like souls, without body or shape. You must be the pen which gives them that."

– D.K.

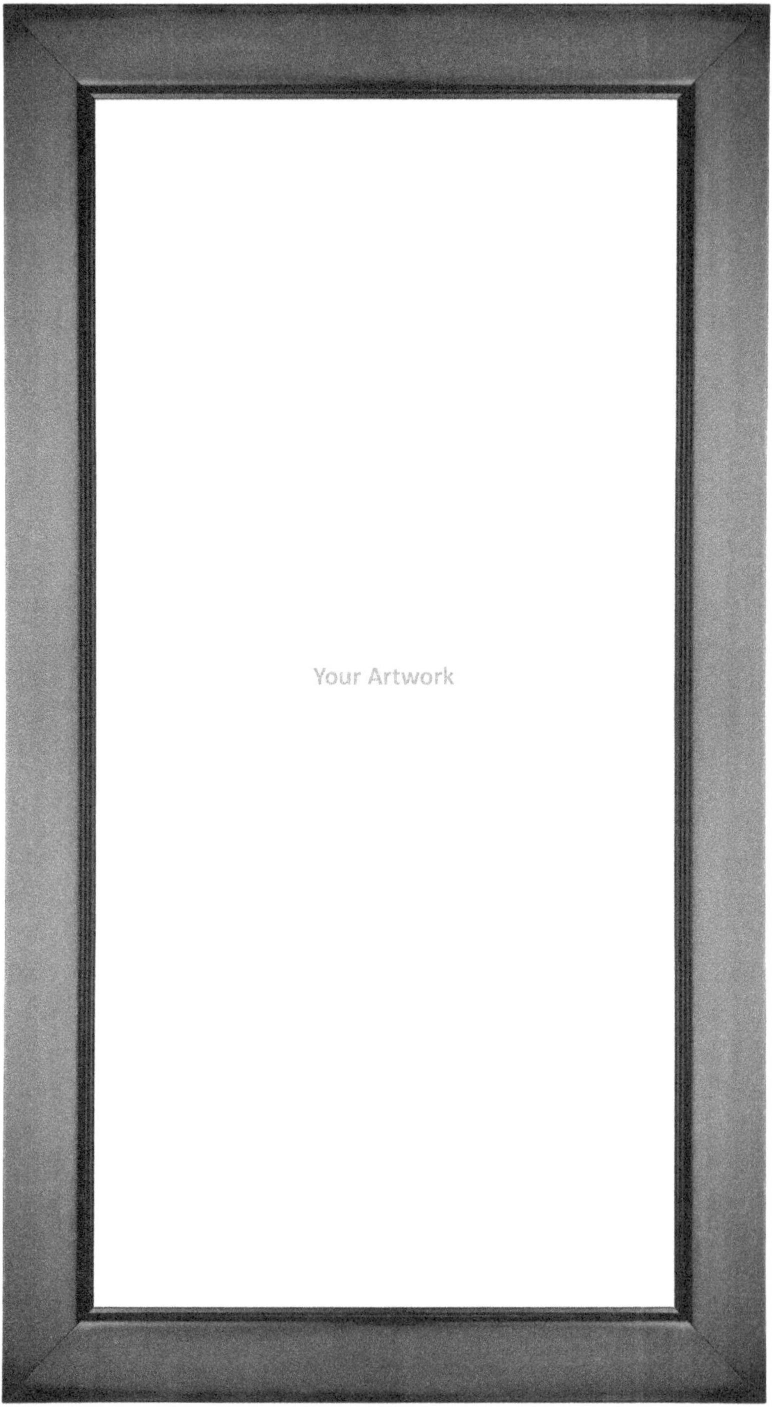
Your Artwork

CHAPTER 5

Chapter Title

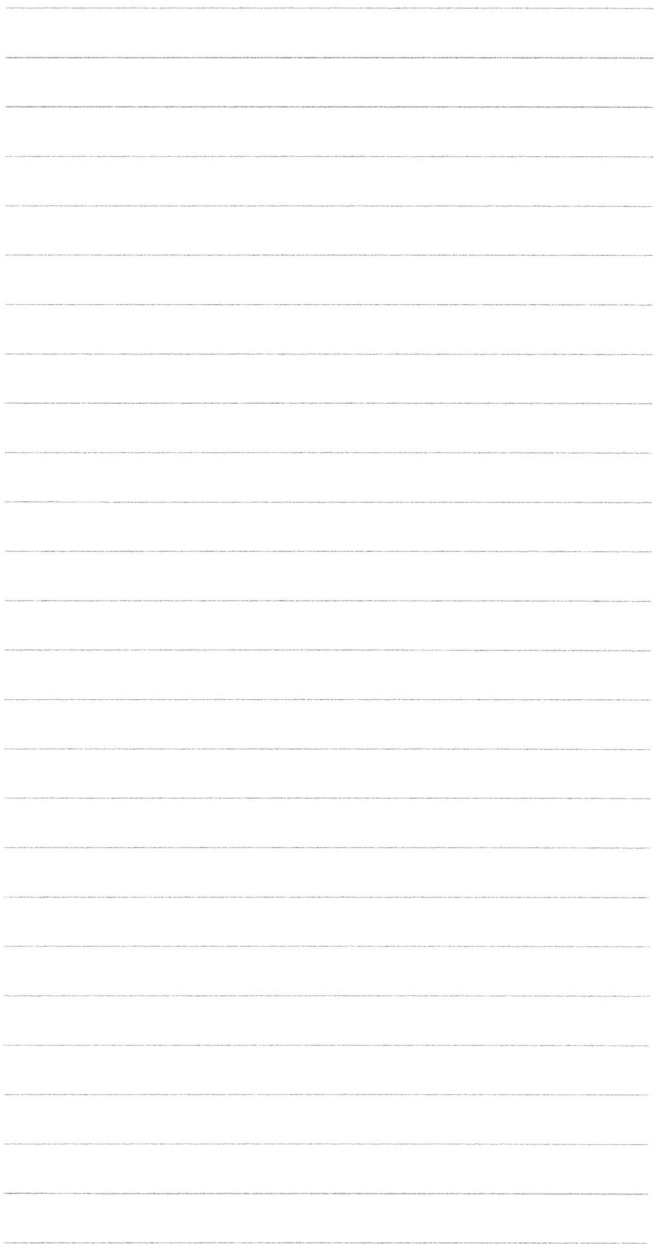

"Success is a journey, not a destination —
half the fun is getting there."

— Gita Bellin

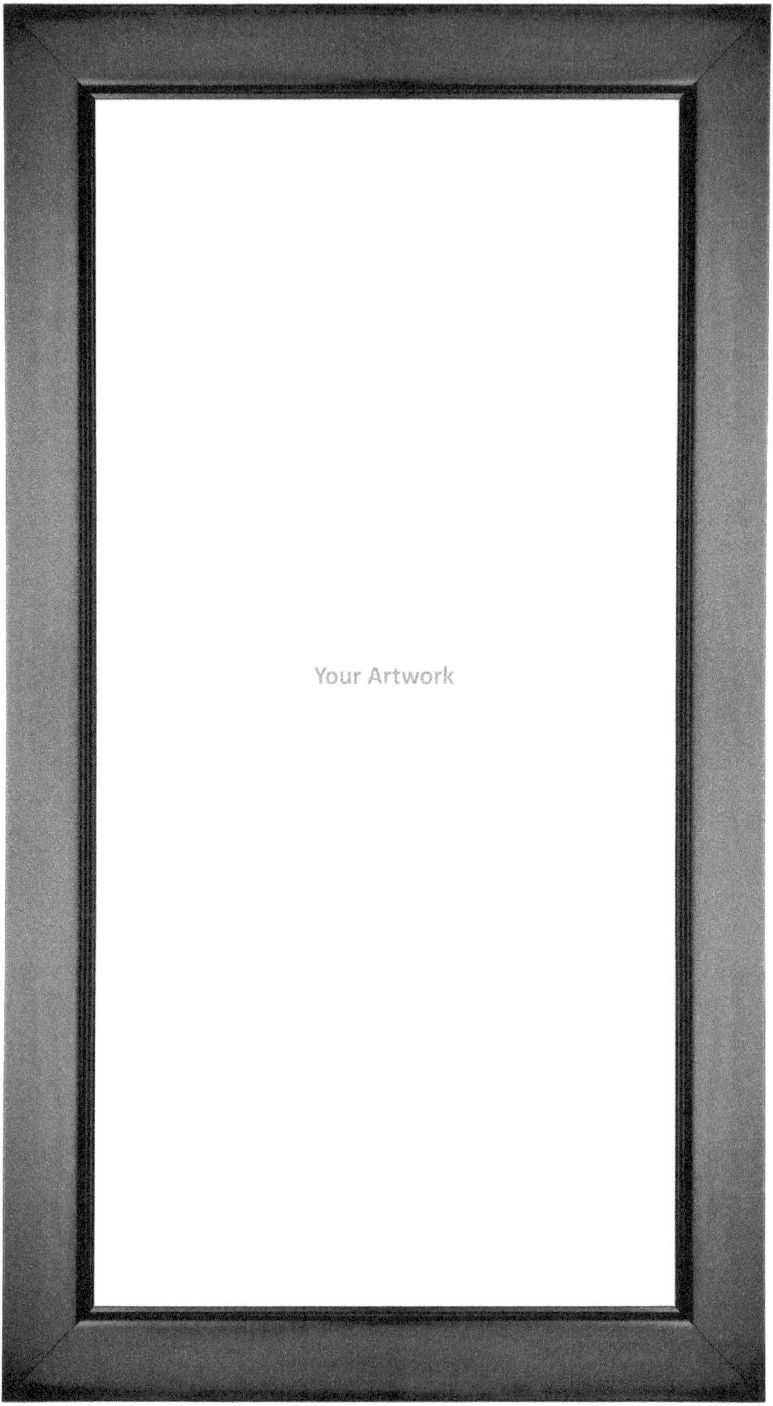
Your Artwork

CHAPTER 6

Chapter Title

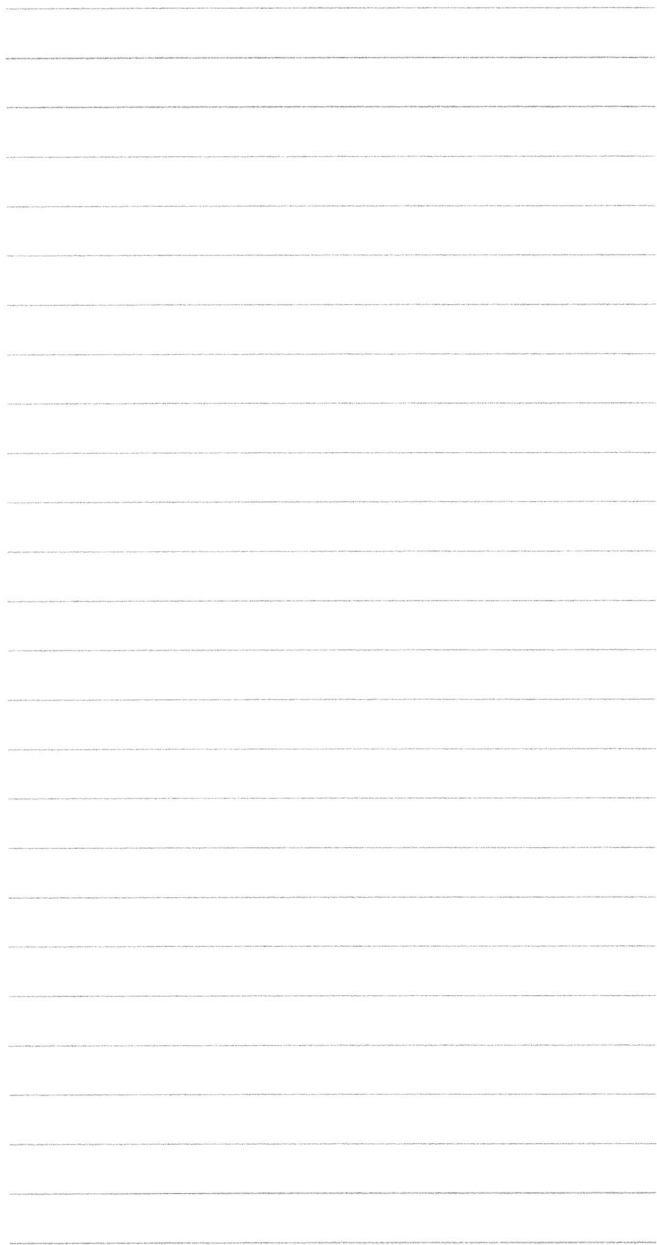

"Never be afraid to tread the path alone.
Go forward with courage and clarity
and you will never be alone."

— D.K.

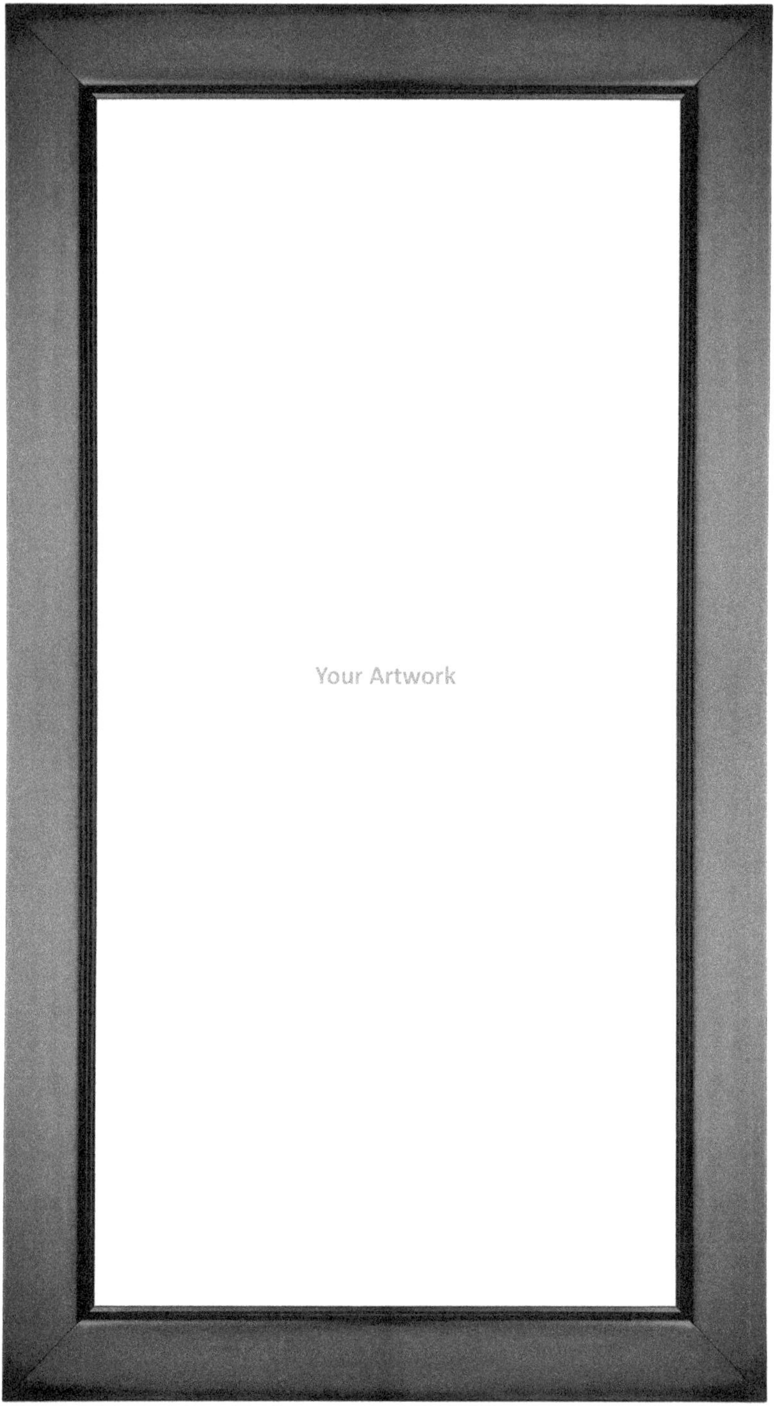
Your Artwork

CHAPTER 7

Chapter Title

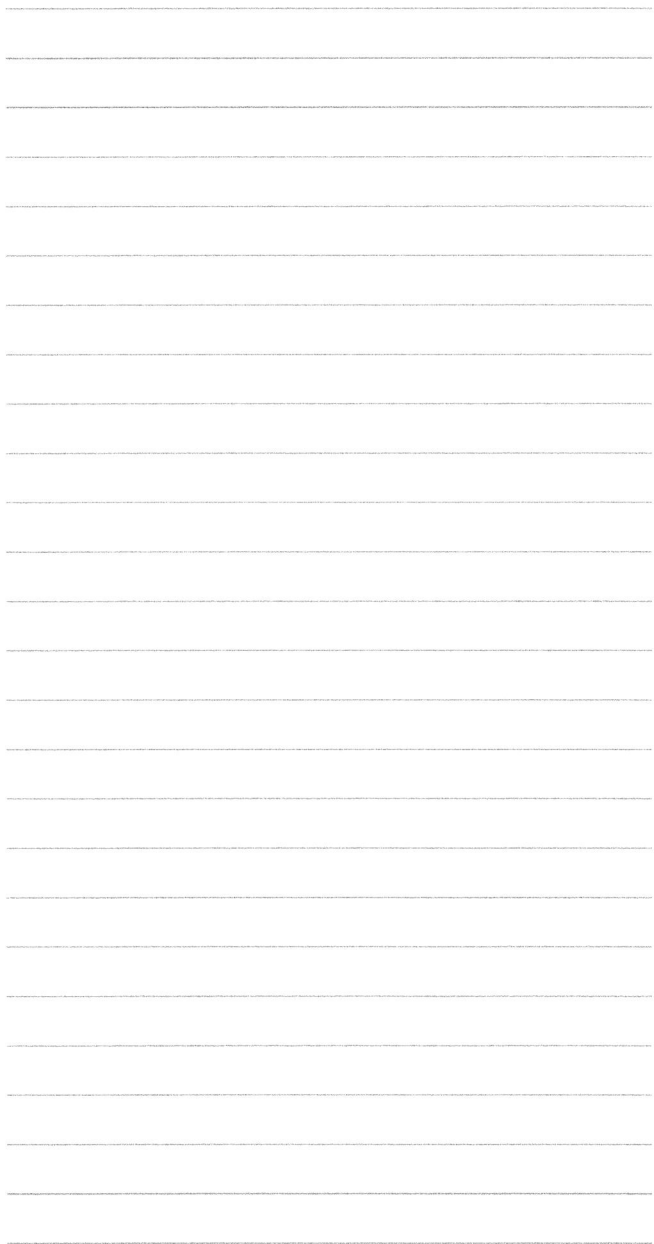

"The story of your characters has already been told.
Their lives were loaded in your pen when you
picked it up; you just need to write them down
so that you can live the story too."

— D.K.

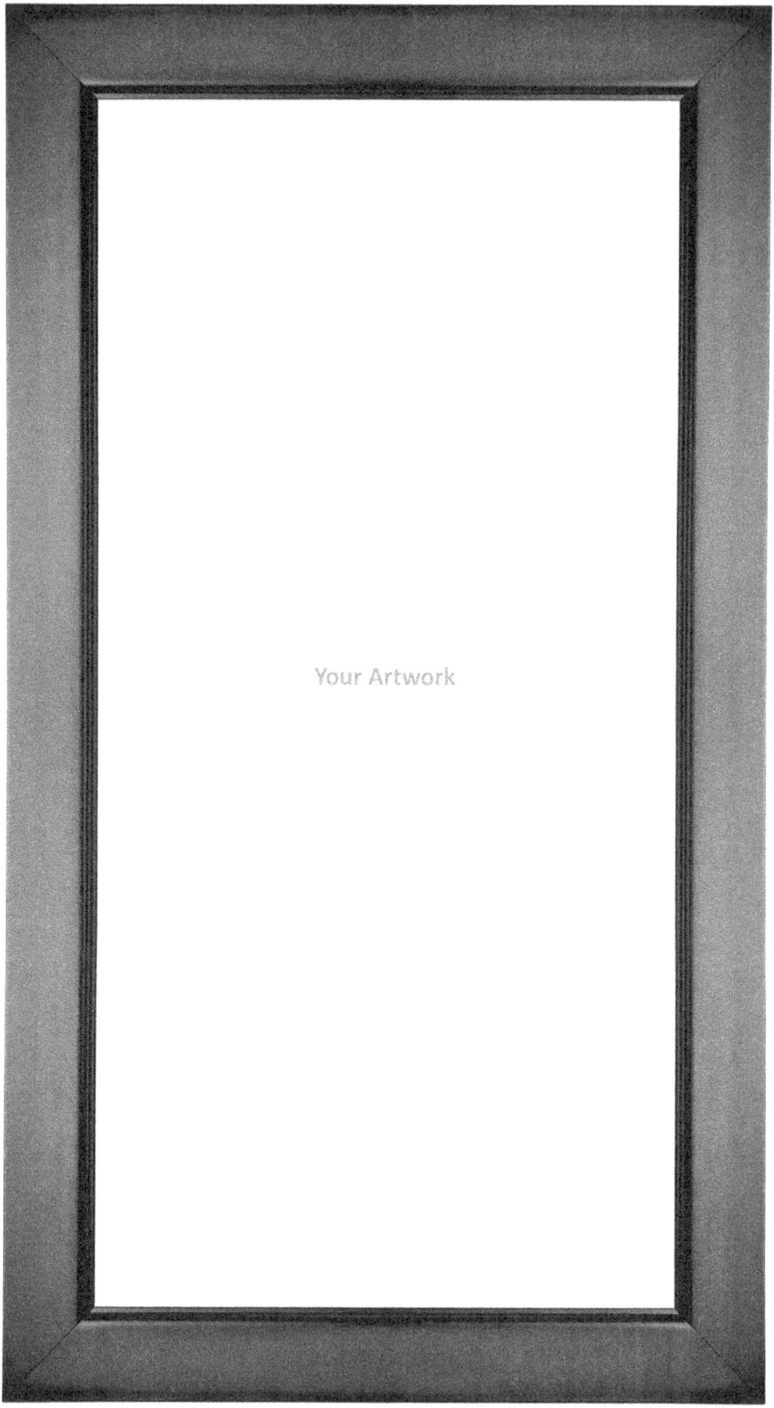
Your Artwork

CHAPTER 8

Chapter Title

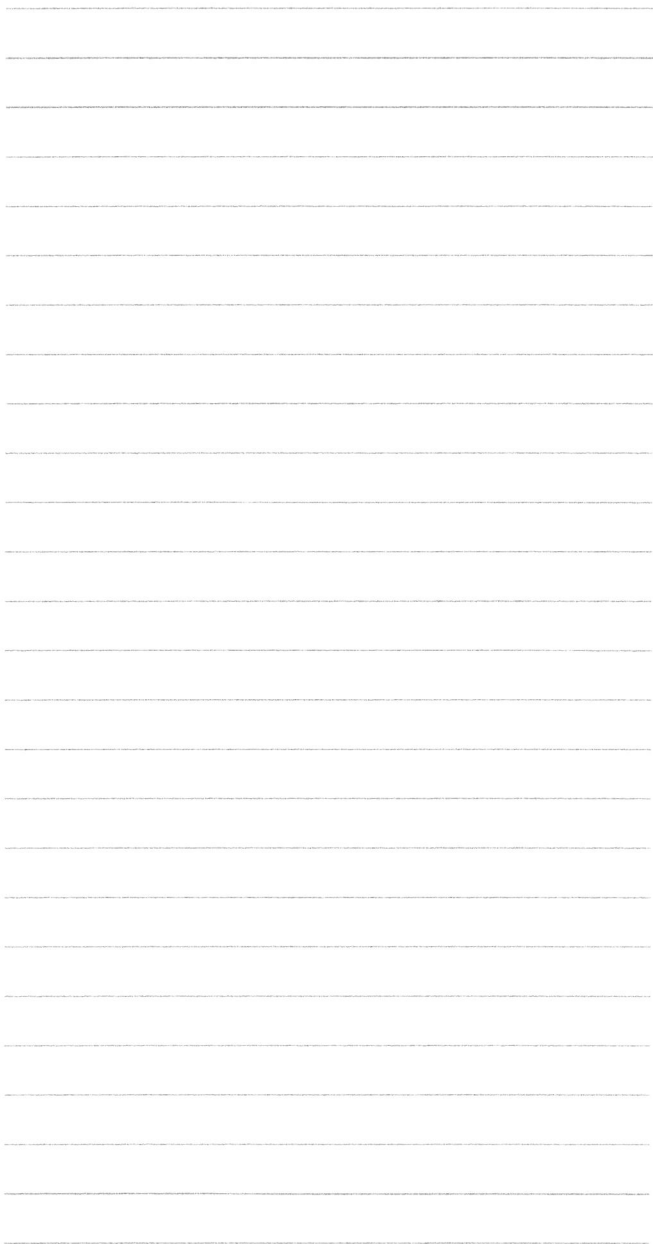

"All the world's a stage." Within these pages is your world, your stage, and everything is set, you merely need to give the characters their cues.

— Shakespeare, D.K.

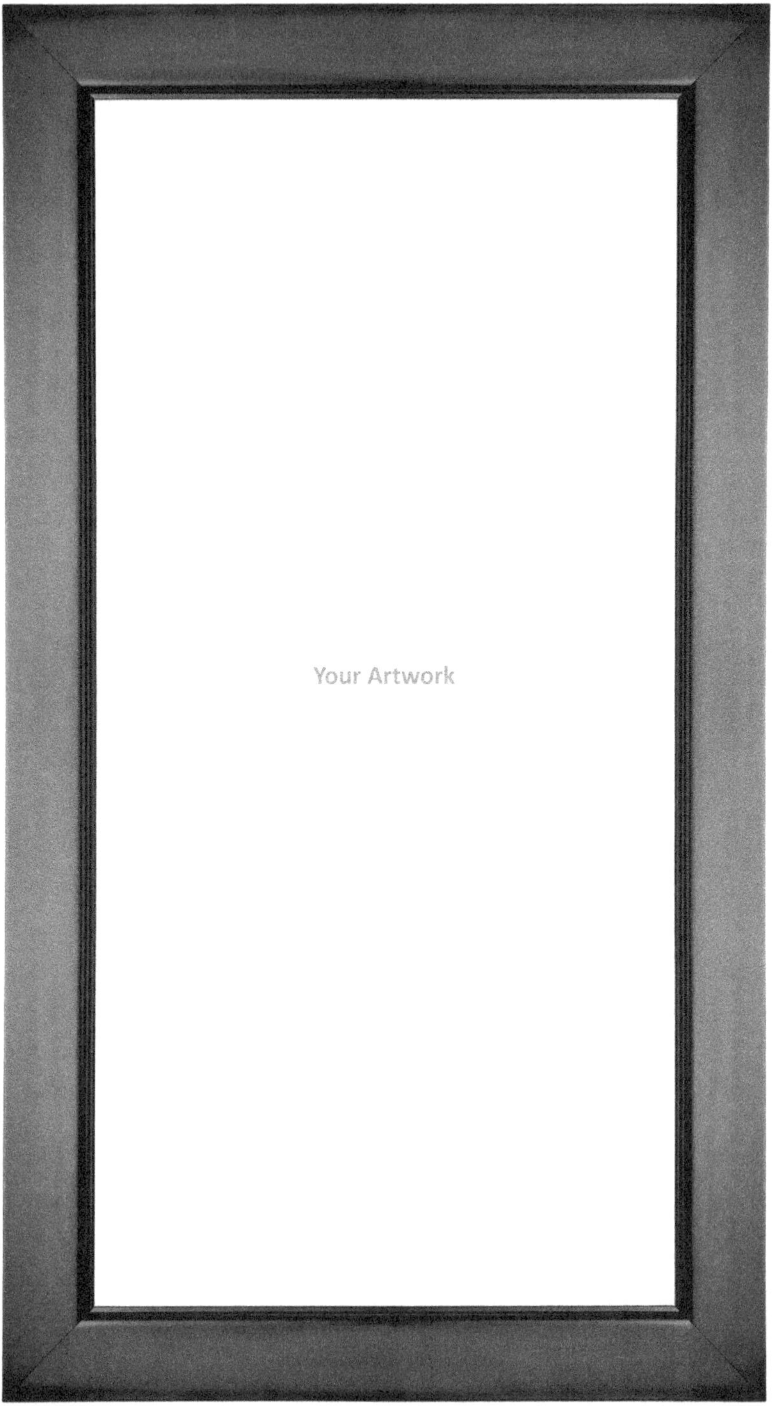
Your Artwork

CHAPTER 9

Chapter Title

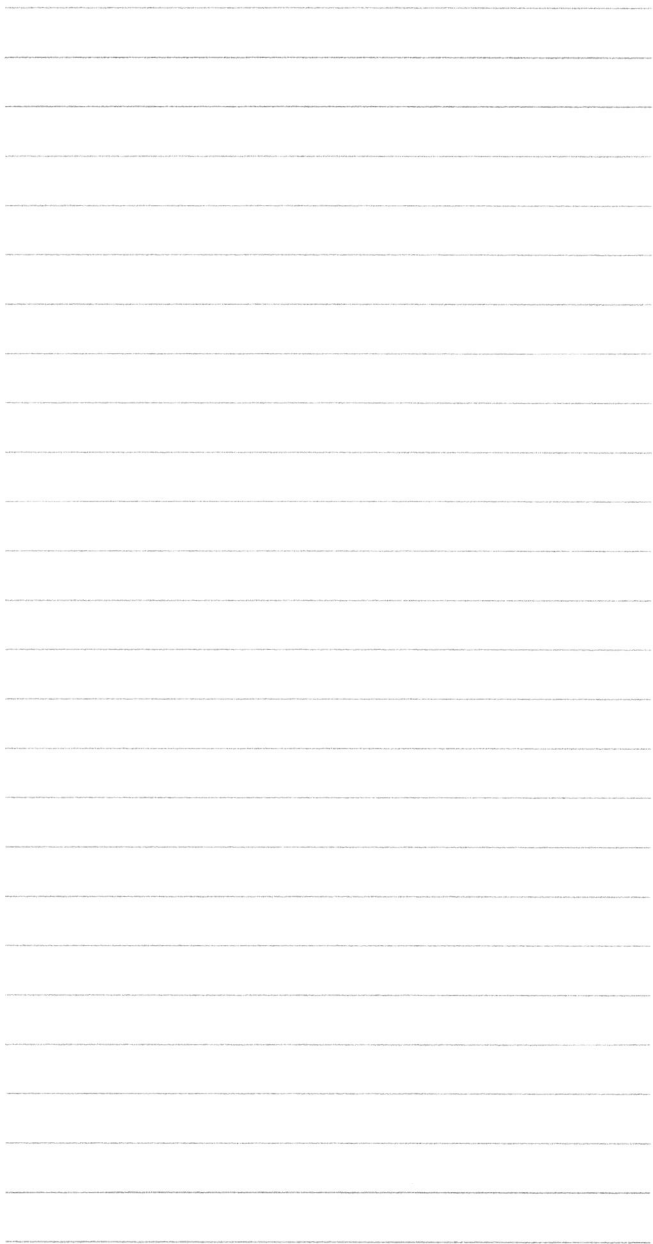

"If you seek immortality, all you need do is bless immortality on someone else."

— D.K.

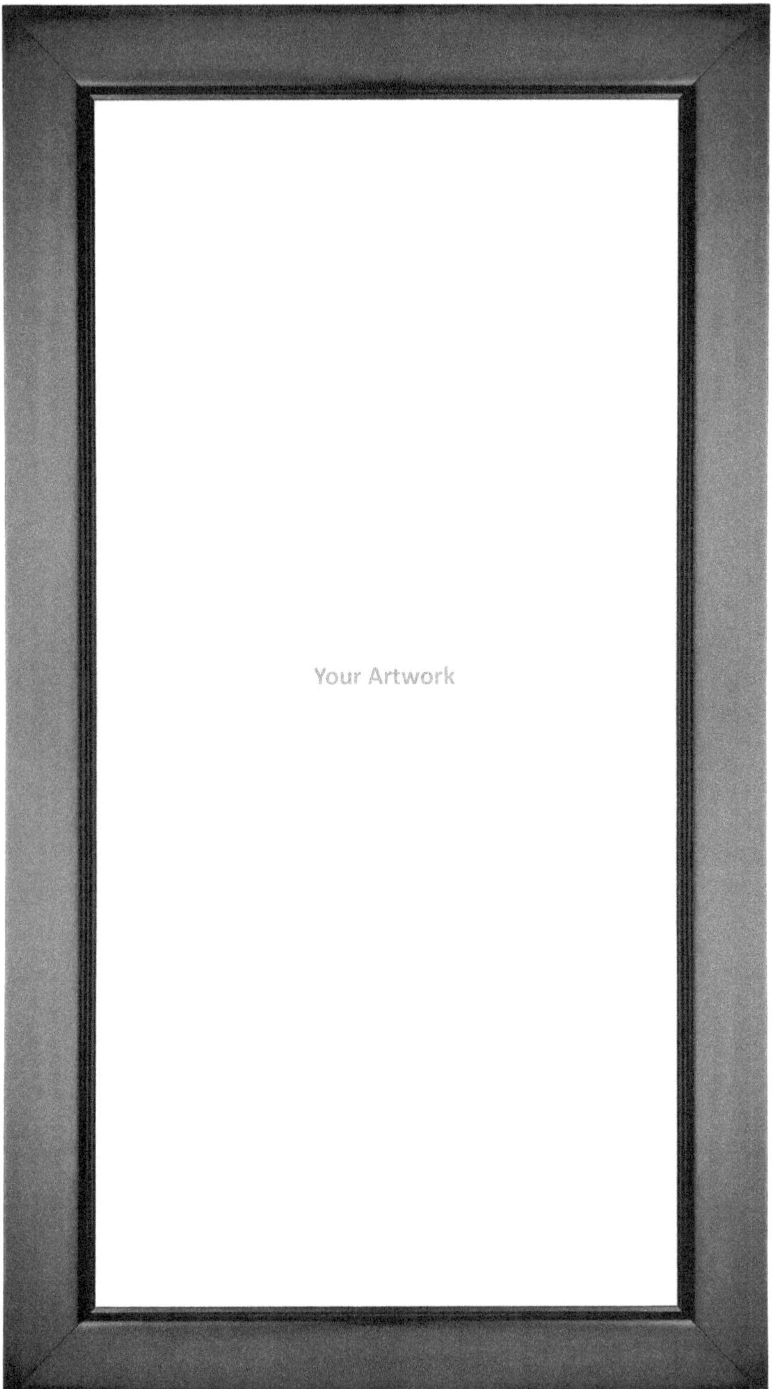
Your Artwork

CHAPTER 10

Chapter Title

74

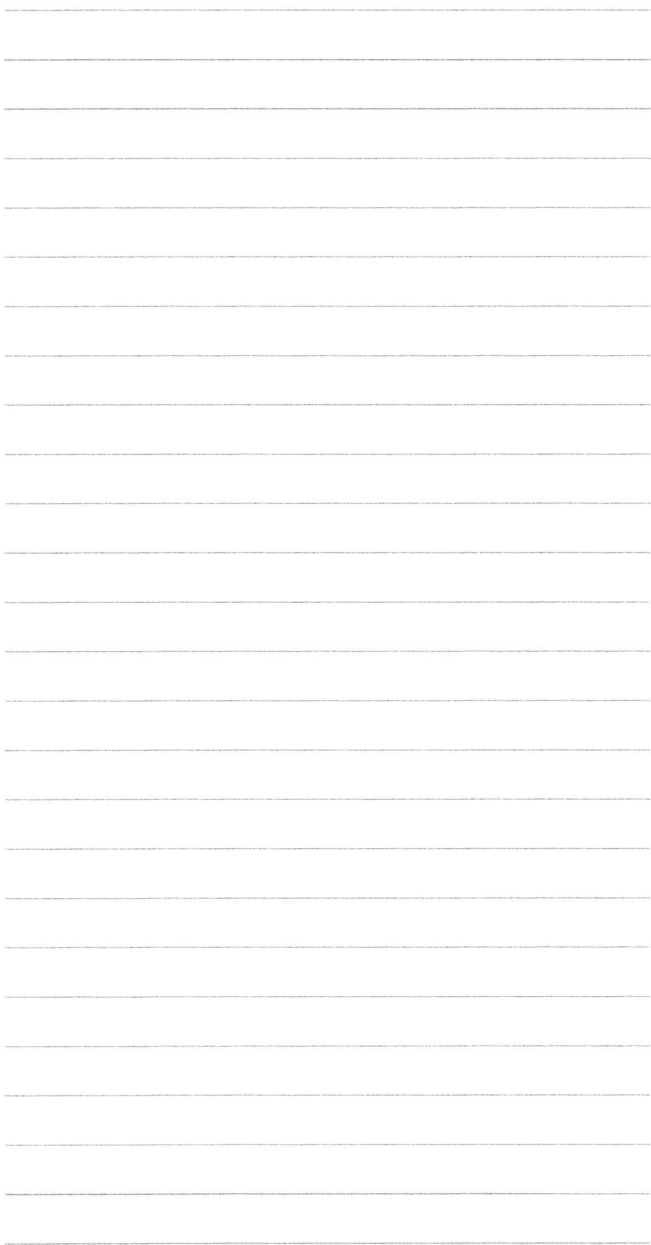

"Life is the perspective of observation."

— D.K.

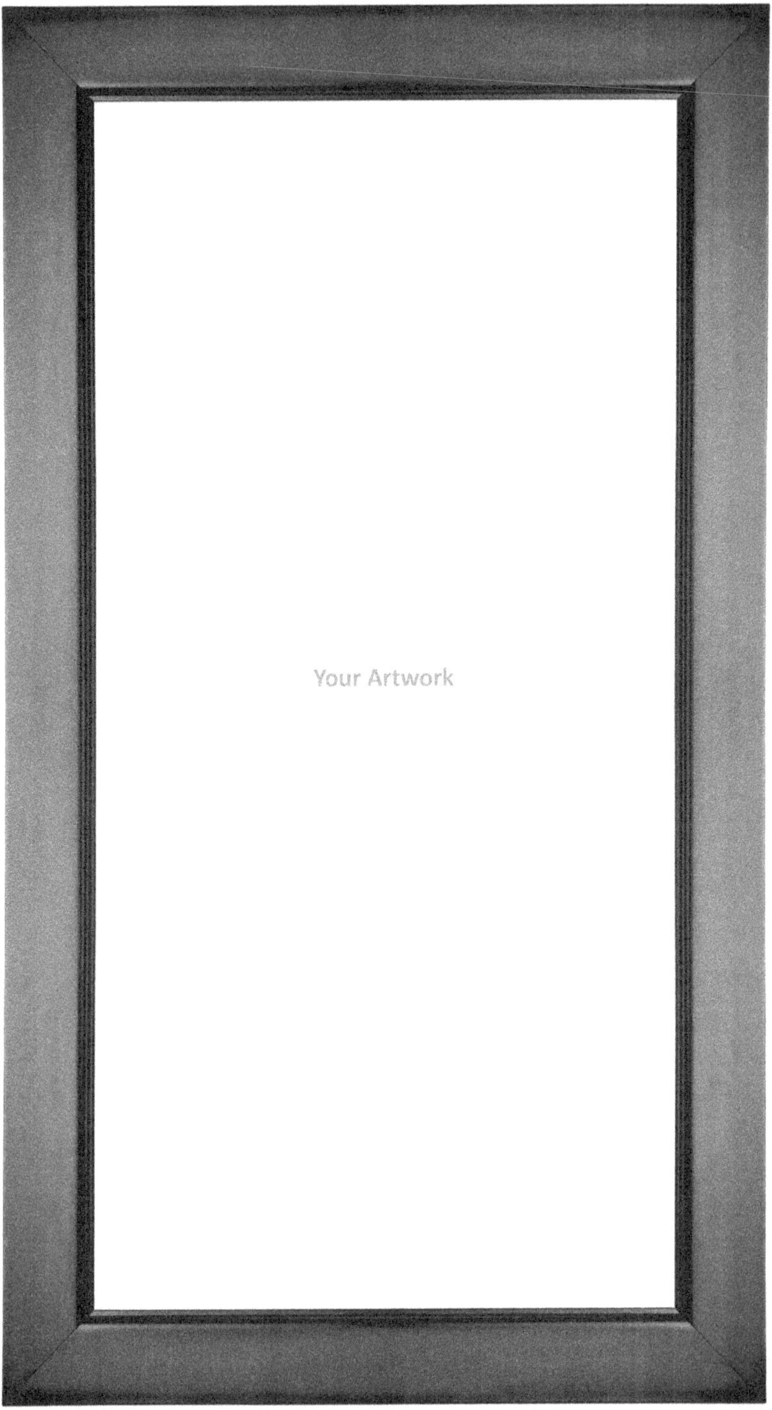
Your Artwork

CHAPTER 11

Chapter Title

82

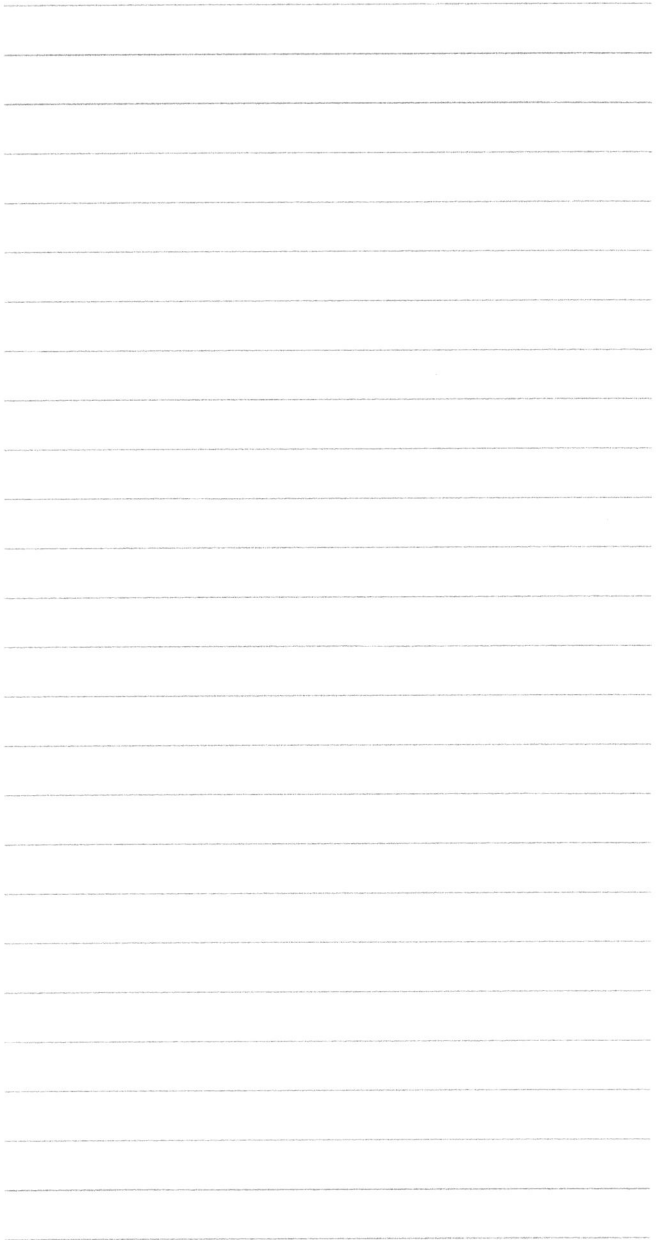

"A person's true character is revealed by what they
do when no one is watching."

– Anonymous

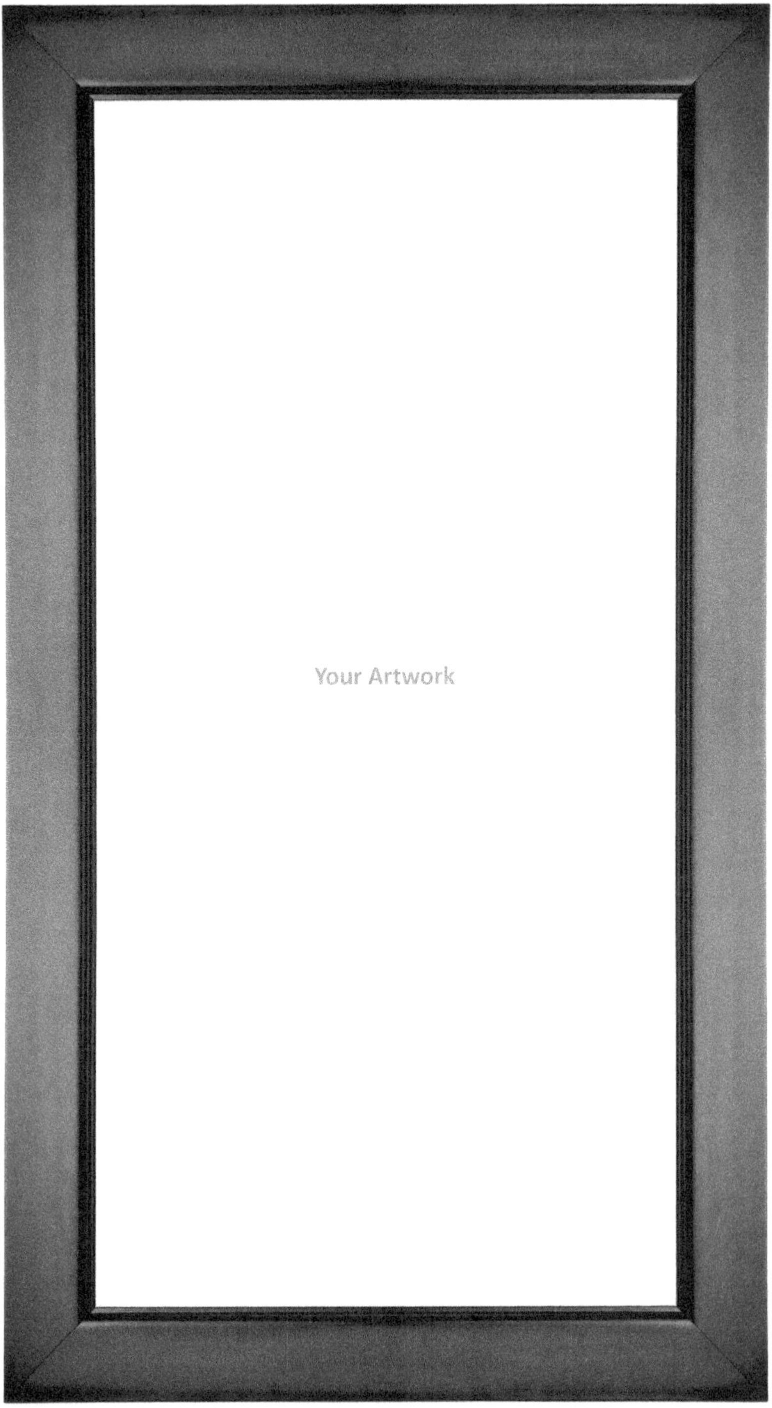
Your Artwork

CHAPTER 12

Chapter Title

"Goals are dreams with deadlines."

-- Anonymous

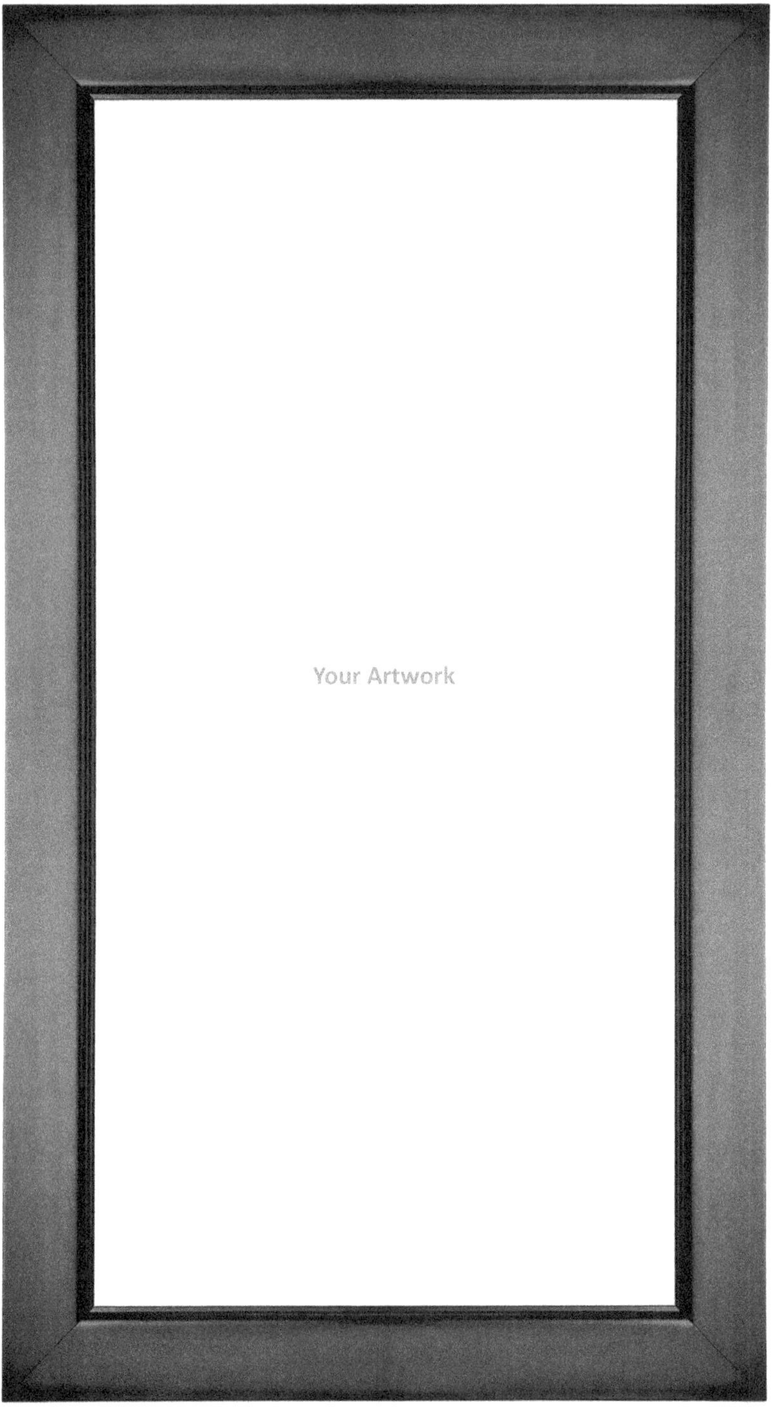
Your Artwork

CHAPTER 13

Chapter Title

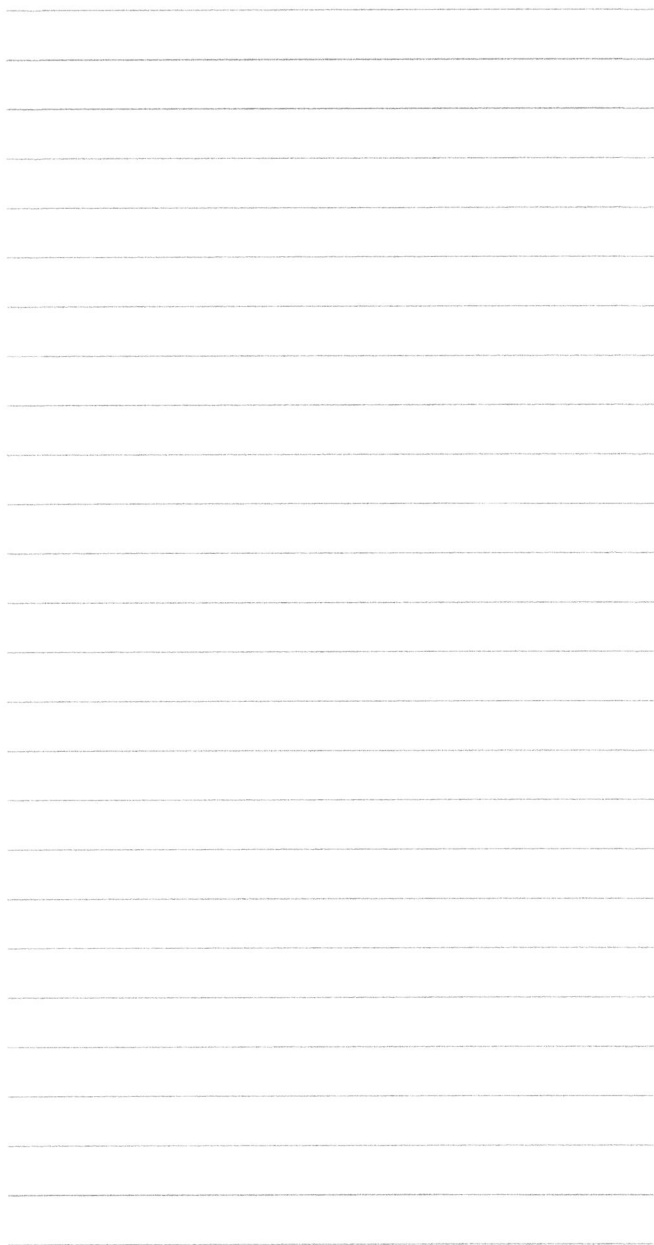

"An artist is not paid for their labor
but for their vision."

– Anonymous

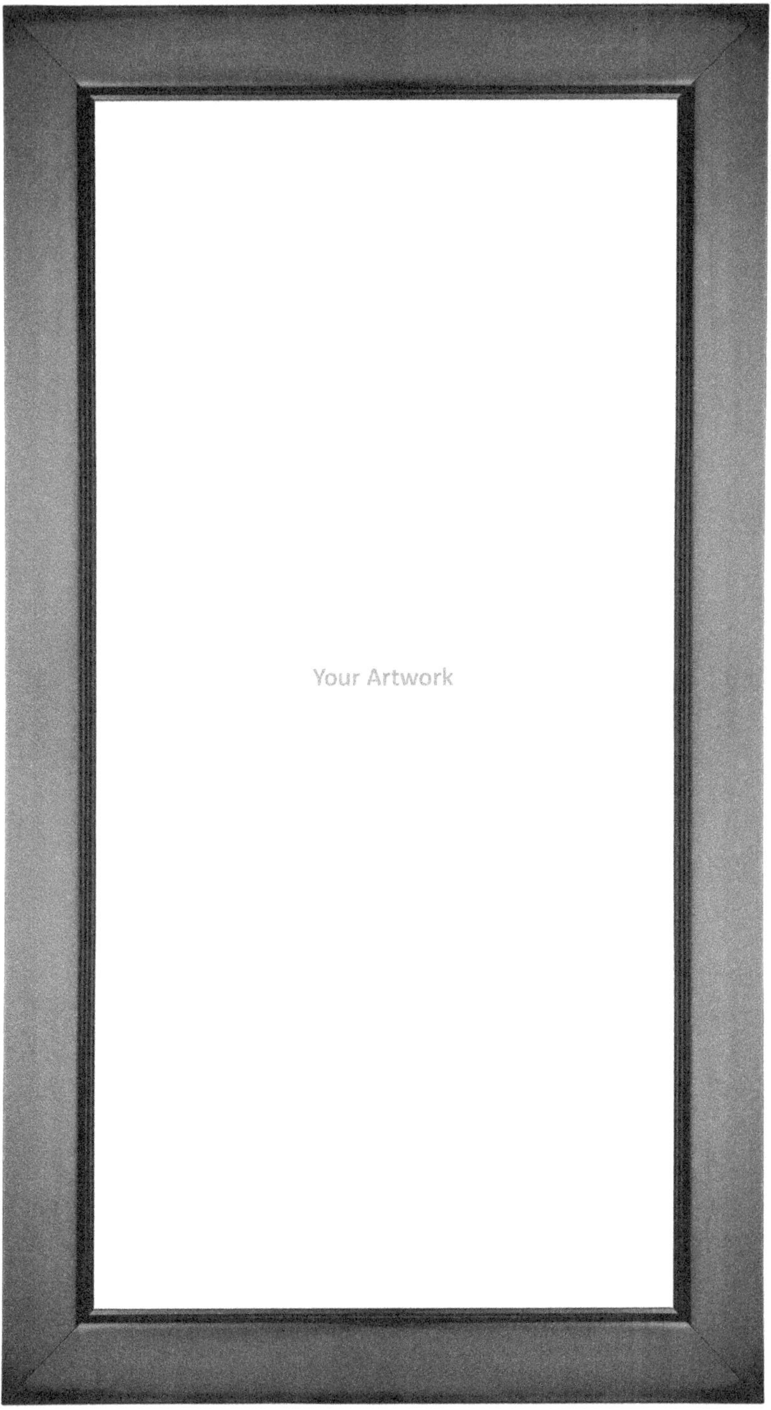
Your Artwork

CHAPTER 14

Chapter Title

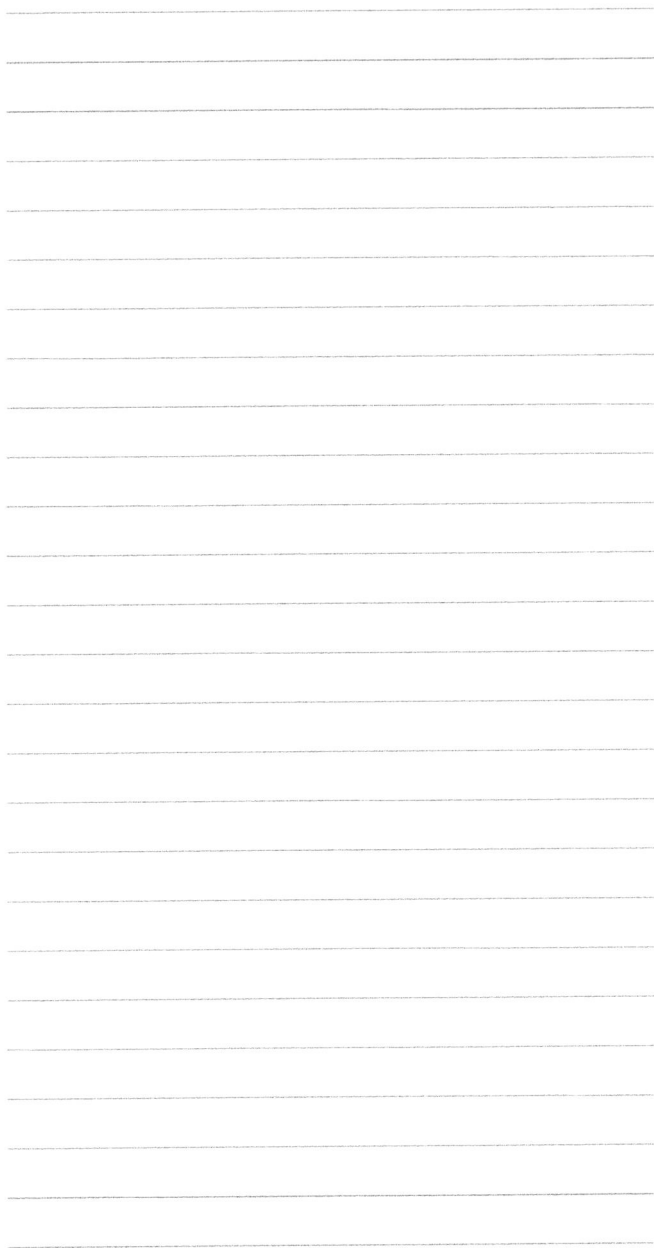

"Every artist dips their brush in their own soul and paints their own nature into their pictures."

— Anonymous

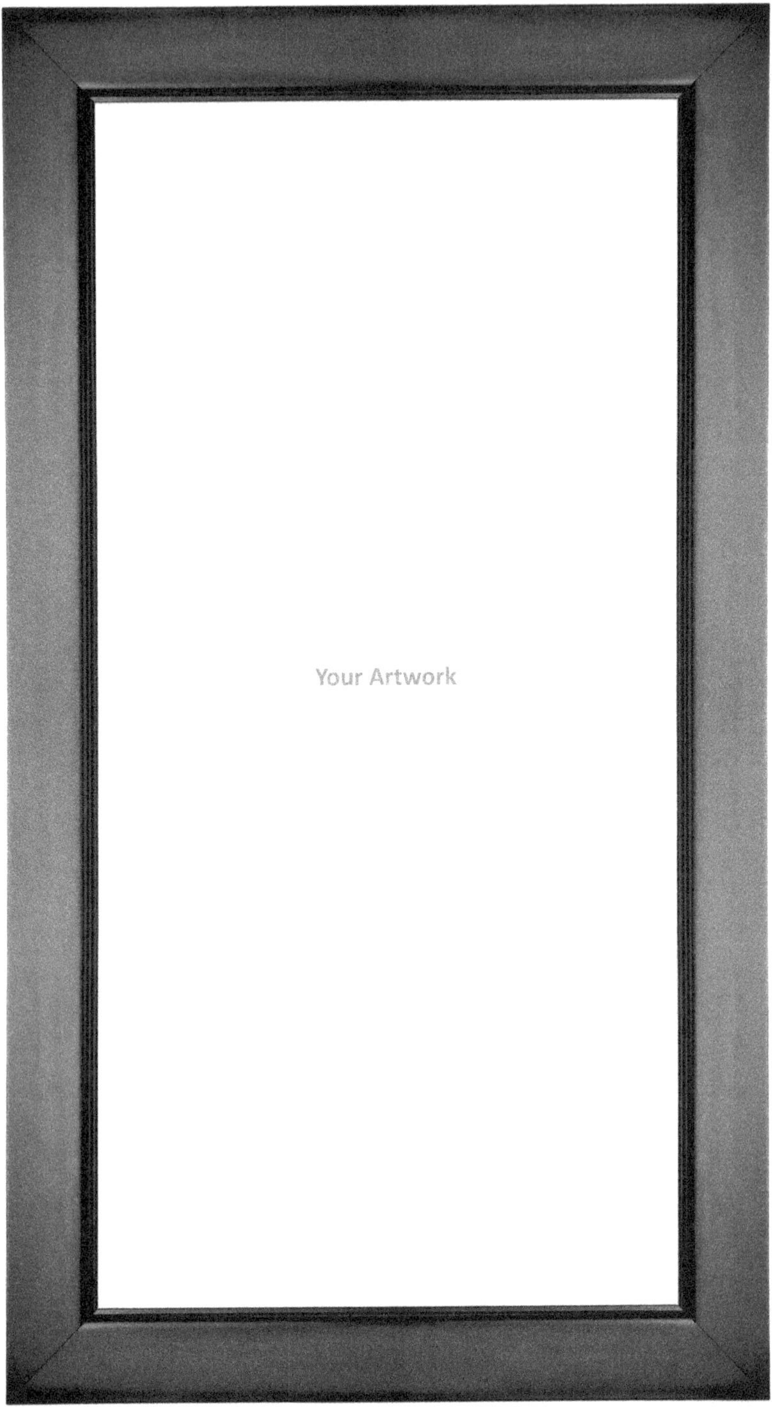
Your Artwork

CHAPTER 15

Chapter Title

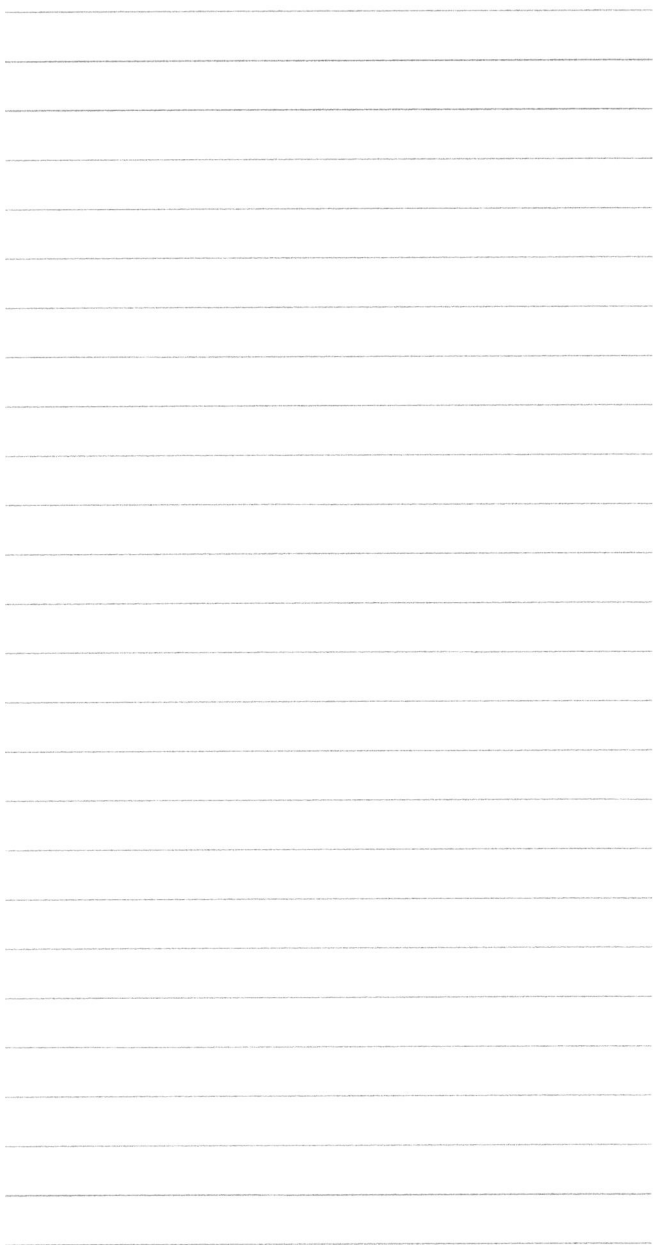

"What garlic is to food, insanity is to art."

— Anonymous

Your Artwork

CHAPTER 16

Chapter Title

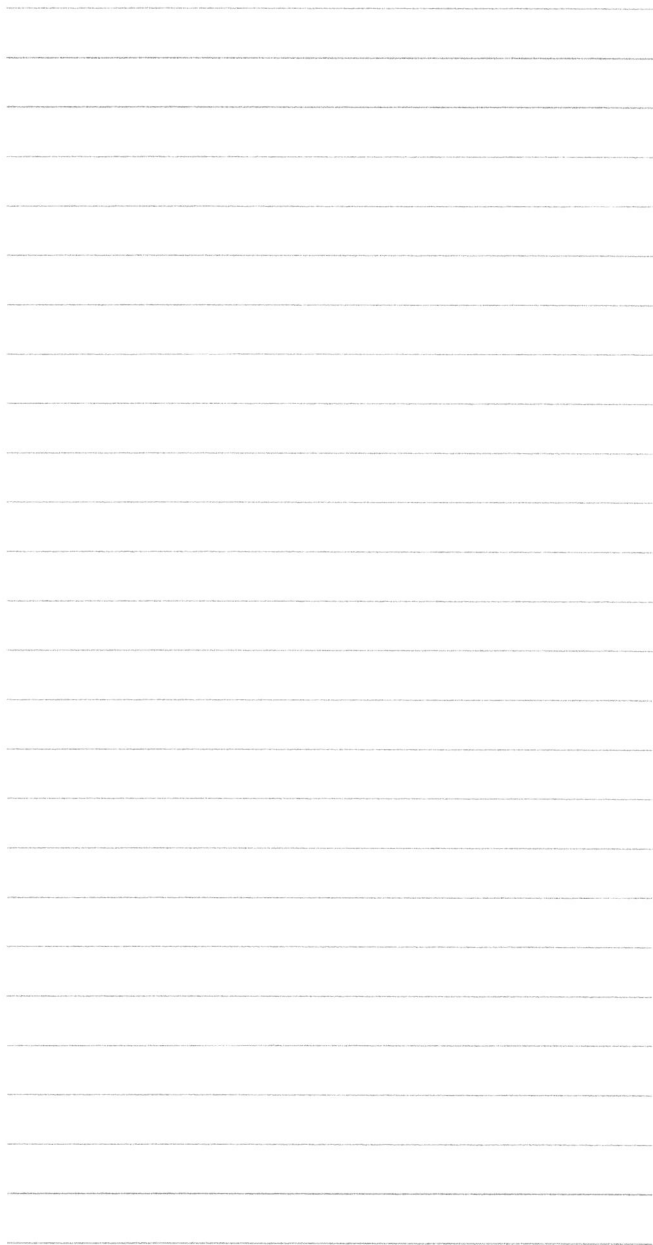

"Tension is who you think you should be,
relaxation is who you are. Relax, then what you
create will be truly yours."

– Anonymous

CHAPTER 17

Chapter Title

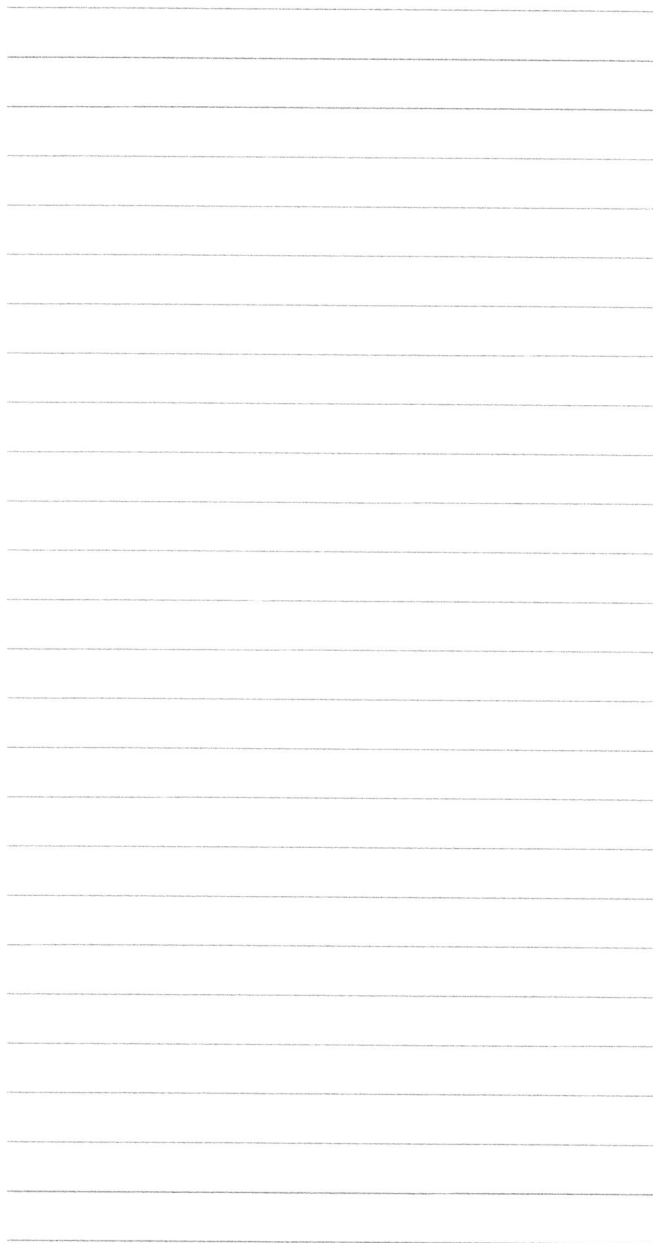

134

"There is a fountain of youth;
It is the imagination of your mind."

– D.K.

CHAPTER 18

Chapter Title

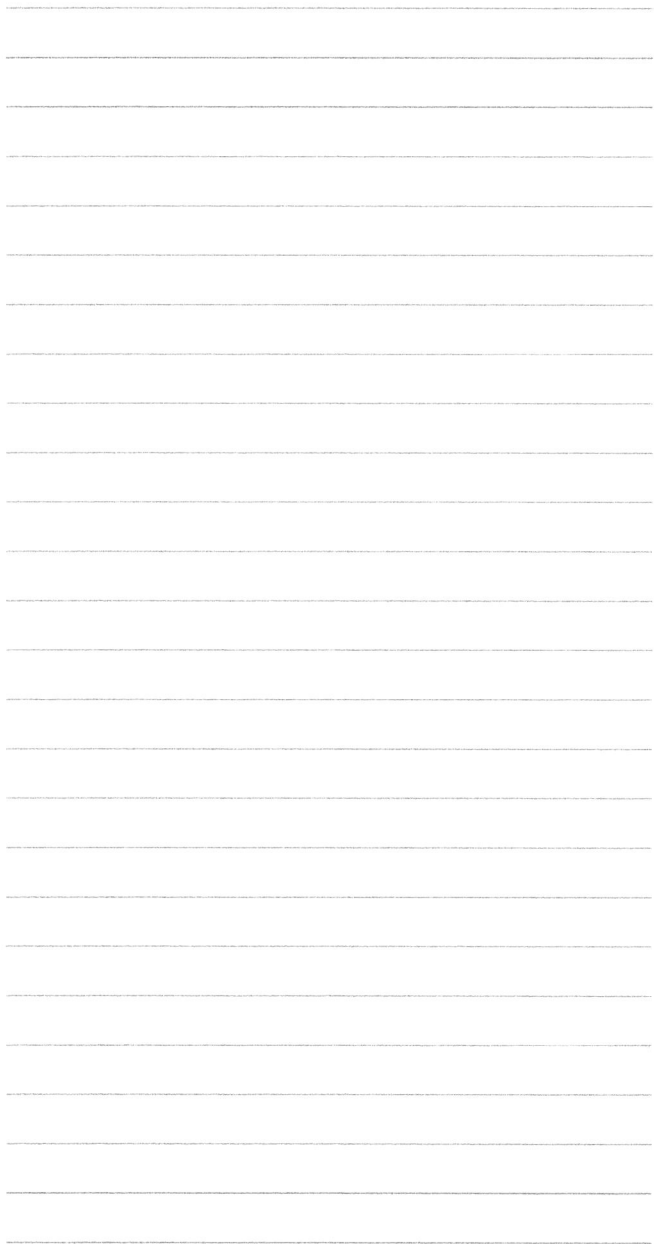

"Just like painting, writing starts with a blank canvas or page. It is what we bring to it that makes for beauty and pleasure."

-- Vicki Easingwood

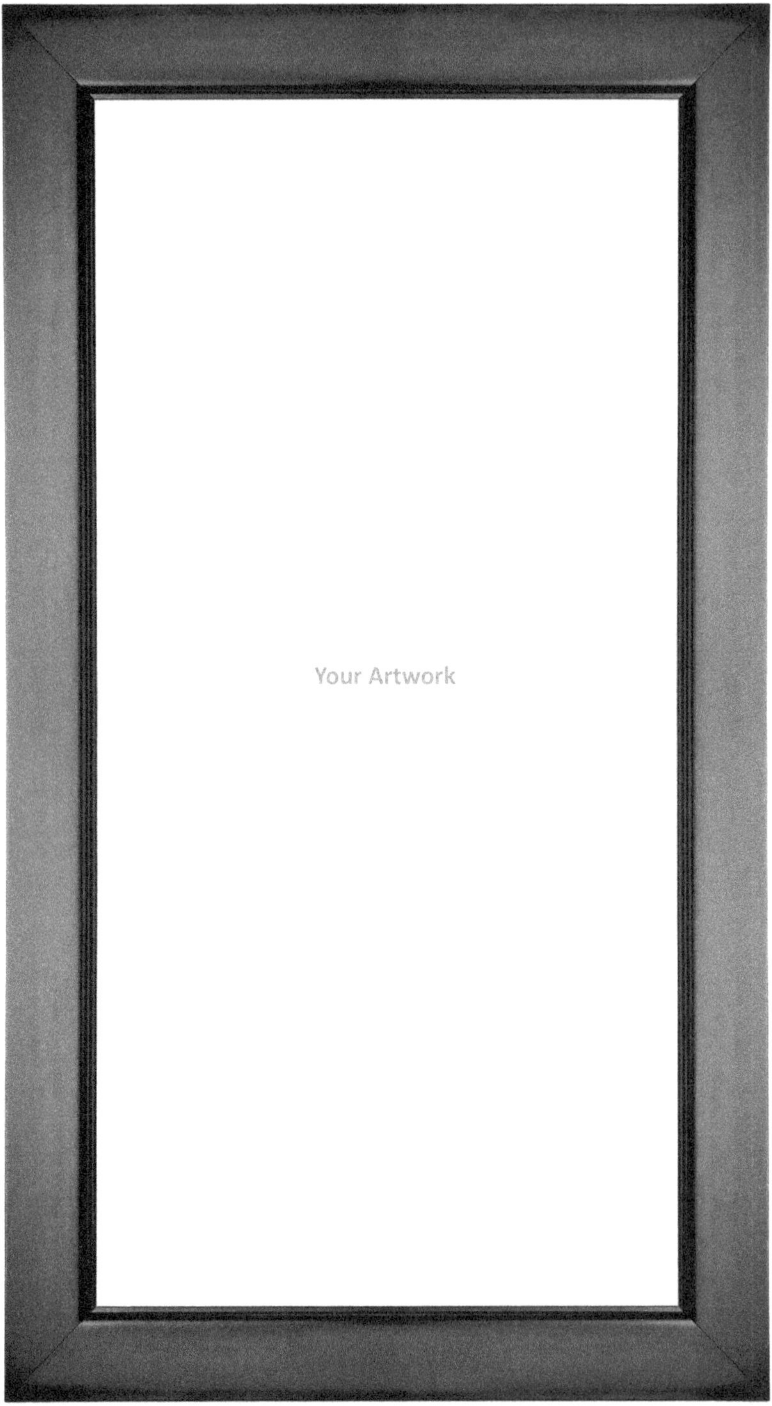
Your Artwork

CHAPTER 19

Chapter Title

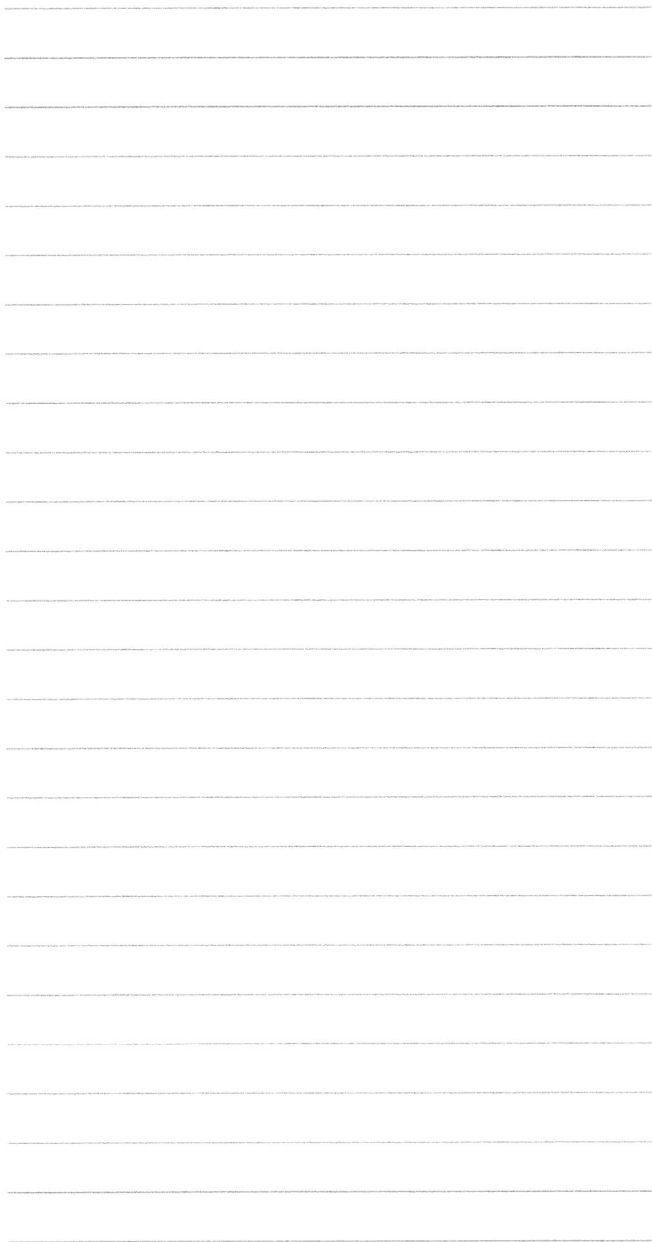

"It's the writing that teaches you."

– Isaac Asimov

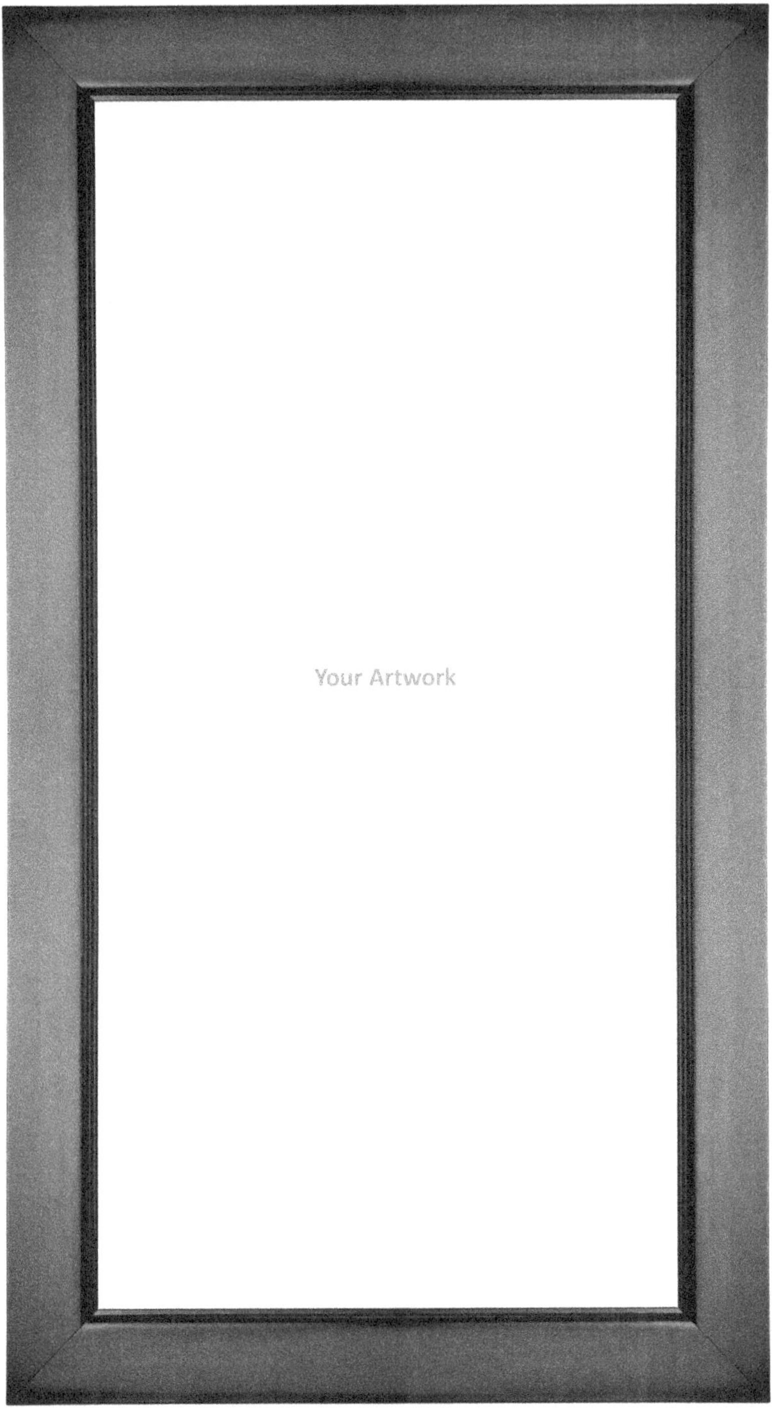
Your Artwork

CHAPTER 20

Chapter Title

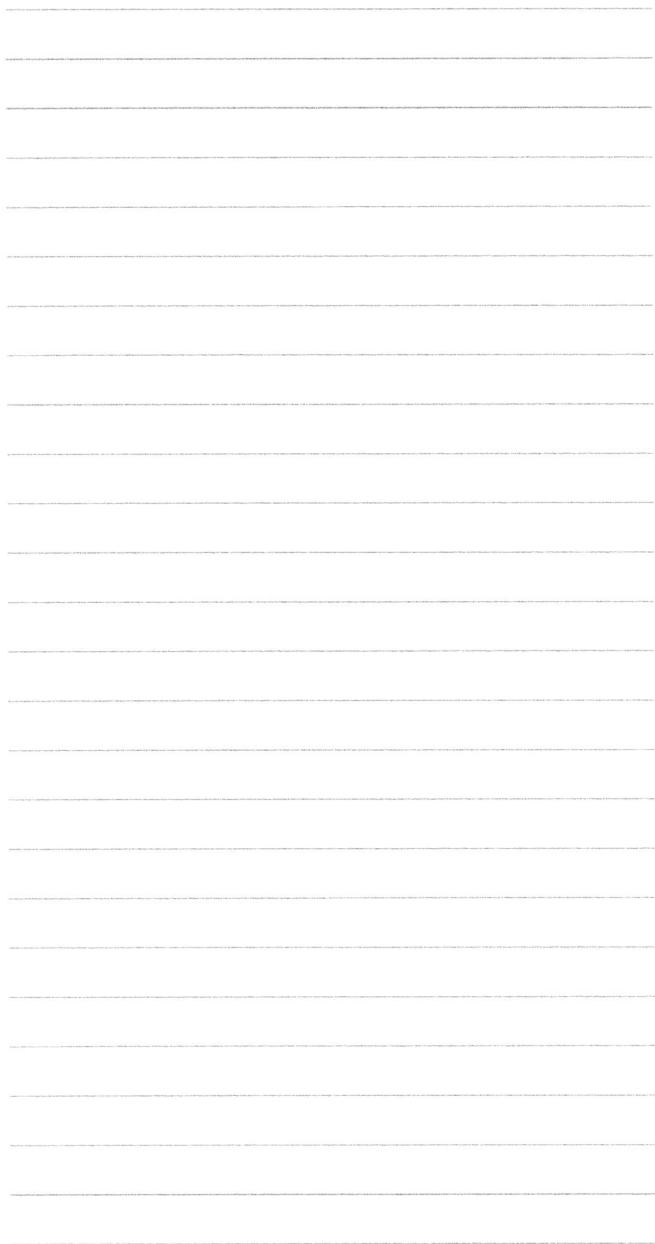

"Writing is worthwhile because it gives us to ourselves,
and then to each other."

— Cathleen Rountree

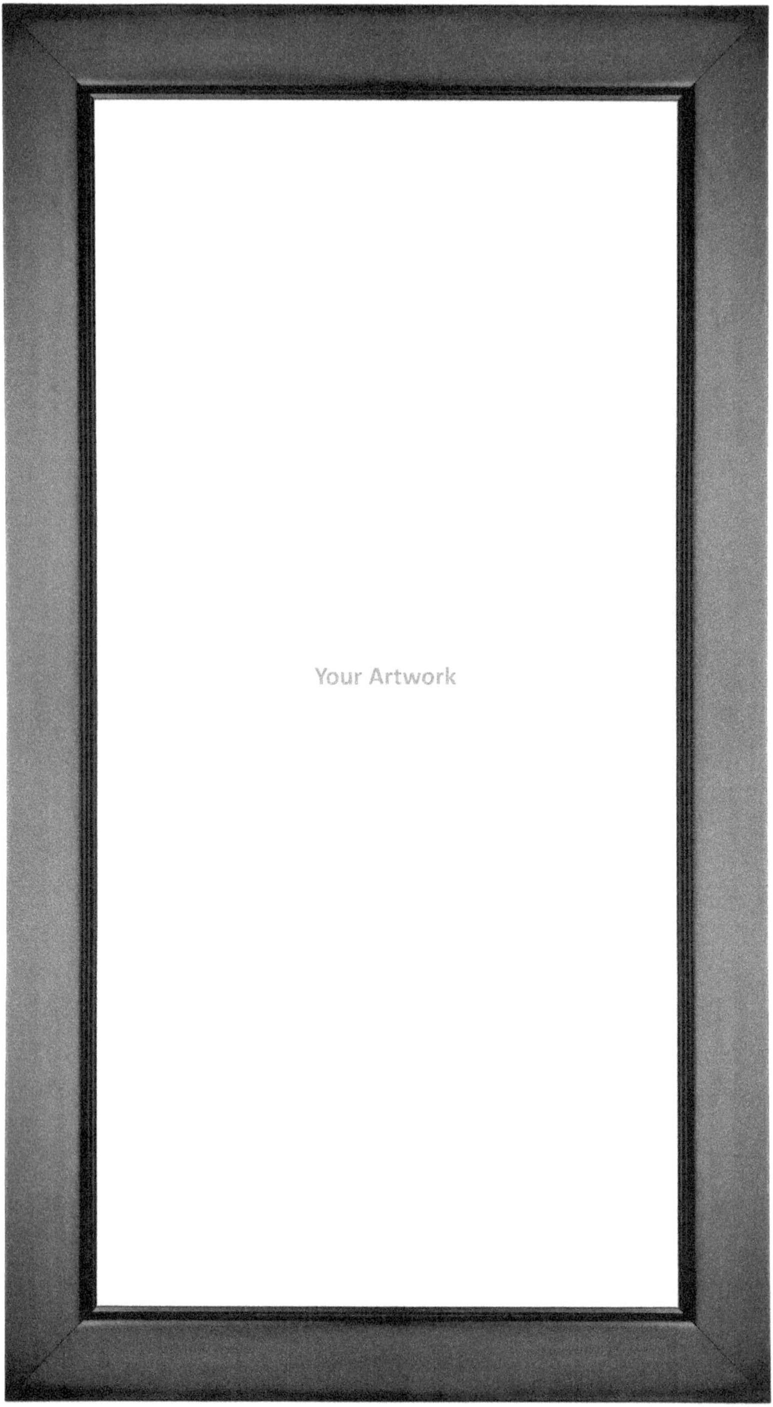
Your Artwork

CHAPTER 21

Chapter Title

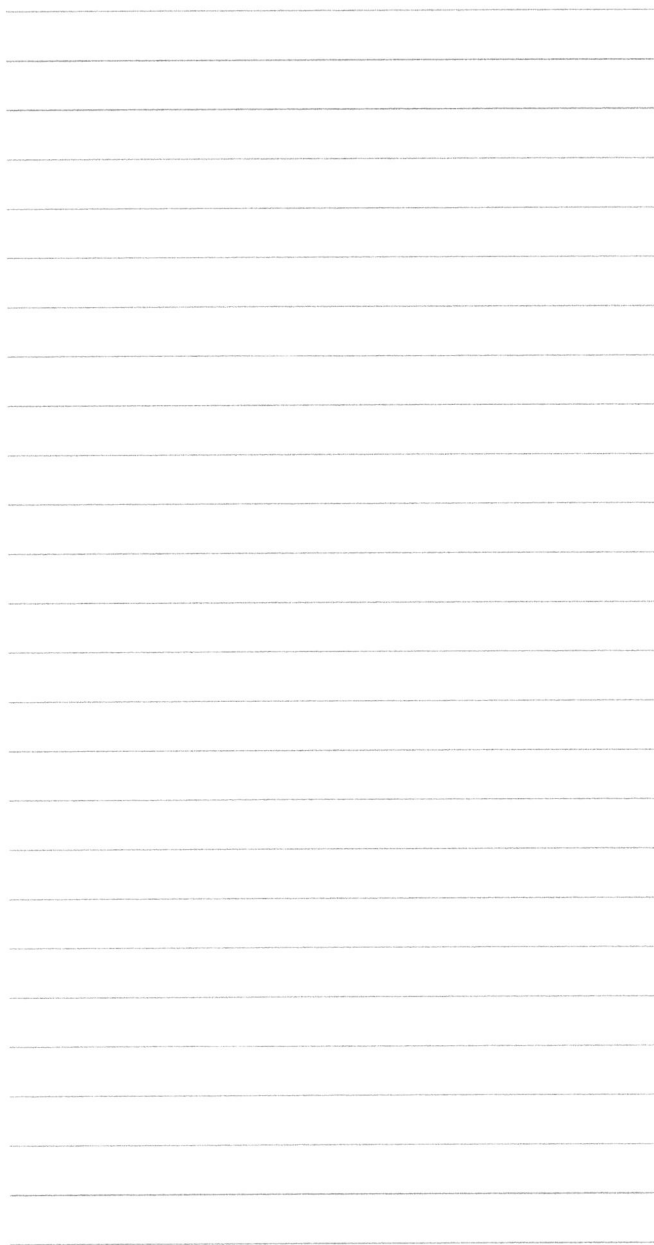

"It is good to have an end to journey towards;
but it is the journey that matters in the end."

– Ursula K. Leguin

THE

END

OR NOT

IMAGINATION SPILL-OVER

What's Next?

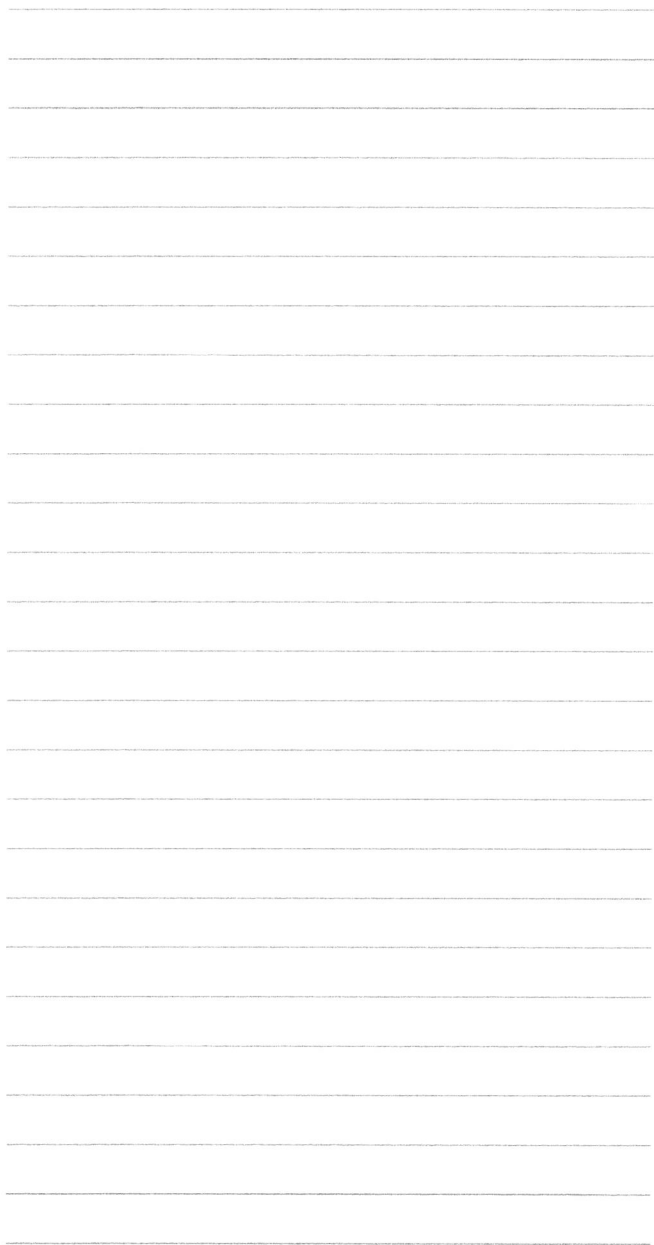

BACK COVER

Your Photo

Your Bio

Order another copy of **The Invisible Story** to continue the adventure or to start a new one.

www.ingramcontent.com/pod-product-compliance
Lightning Source LLC
Chambersburg PA
CBHW031317040426
42443CB00005B/111